Table Of Contents

Preface

In a world filled with uncertainty, chaos, and confusion, the need for faith is greater than ever. As men, we are constantly faced with challenges and obstacles that test our resolve, strength, and beliefs. It is during these trying times that we must turn to the examples set forth by the faithful men in the Bible.

"Men of Faith" is a book that delves into the lives of some of the most courageous, steadfast, and unwavering men in the Bible. From Noah, who built an ark against all odds, to David, who defeated Goliath with just a stone and a sling, these men exemplify what it means to have faith in the face of adversity.

Throughout the pages of this book, you will discover the stories of men like Abraham, who left his homeland to follow God's call, and Joseph, who remained faithful despite being sold into slavery by his own brothers. These men faced tremendous trials and tribulations, yet their faith never wavered.

But "Men of Faith" is not just a collection of stories from the Bible. It is a call to action for men everywhere to grow in their faith, to trust in God's plan, and to live a life of purpose and meaning. Each chapter in this book is filled with lessons, insights, and wisdom that will inspire and challenge you to become a man of faith.

As you embark on this journey through the lives of these faithful men, I encourage you to reflect on your own faith journey. What obstacles are standing in the way of your growth? What fears are holding you back from fully trusting in God's plan for your life? It is my hope that "Men of Faith" will ignite a fire within you to pursue a deeper relationship with God and to live out your faith in a bold and courageous way.

I believe that now, more than ever, the world needs men of faith. Men who are willing to take a stand for what is right, who are unafraid to speak the truth, and who rely on God's strength in times of weakness. It is my prayer that this book will empower you to be that kind of man – a man of faith who can change the world for the better.

So, I invite you to journey through the pages of "Men of Faith" with an open heart and a willing spirit. Allow the stories of these faithful men to inspire and guide you on your own faith journey. May you be challenged, encouraged, and transformed as you seek to grow in your faith and become the man that God has called you to be.

In closing, I leave you with the words of Hebrews 11:1 – "Now faith is confidence in what we hope for and assurance about what we do not see." May the stories of the men of faith in this book remind you that with God, all things are possible. May your faith be strengthened, your resolve solidified, and your heart filled with courage as you embark on this journey of growth and transformation.

May you be a man of faith, now and forevermore.

-    Dr. Brandon Stewart

Chapter 1

What is Faith?

Faith is a central theme in the Christian belief system. It is defined as the confidence in what we hope for and assurance about what we do not see (Hebrews 11:1). Faith is not just a feeling or a belief, but an active trust in God and His promises. In this first chapter of "Men of Faith", we will explore the question of what faith truly is and why it is essential for the Christian walk.

Defining Faith:

Many people have their own interpretations of what faith means. Some see it as blind trust or wishful thinking, while others view it as a logical decision based on evidence. However, in the context of Christianity, faith is much more profound. It goes beyond mere belief in the existence of God and extends to trusting His character and His promises.

Faith is not static; it is dynamic and requires action. James 2:17 tells us that faith without works is dead. In other words, faith should manifest itself in our actions and choices. It is not enough to say we have faith; we must demonstrate it through our deeds.

Another aspect of faith is persistence. Hebrews 11:6 states that without faith, it is impossible to please God, for whoever would draw near to Him must believe that He exists and that He rewards those who seek Him. This verse highlights the importance of continuing to trust God even when we cannot see the outcome. It requires perseverance and a willingness to wait on the Lord's timing.

Faith in God's Promises:

One of the central components of faith is trusting in God's promises. Throughout the Bible, we see examples of men and women who had unwavering faith in God's word. Abraham believed that God would fulfill His promise to make him the father of many nations, even when he and Sarah were well beyond childbearing age (Genesis 15:6).

Moses trusted that God would deliver the Israelites from slavery in Egypt, despite the many obstacles they faced along the way. David had faith that God would protect him from his enemies and establish his kingdom forever. These men of faith were not perfect, but they clung to God's promises and saw them fulfilled in their lives.

As Christians, we have access to the same promises that these men of faith did. We are told in 2 Peter 1:4 that through God's promises, we may become partakers of the divine nature. This means that we can have confidence in God's ability to transform us and fulfill His purposes in our lives.

Faith in the Face of Trials:

Another aspect of faith is trusting God even in the midst of trials and tribulations. Job is a prime example of someone who maintained his faith in God despite losing everything he had. He declared, "Though He slay me, yet will I trust Him" (Job 13:15).

The apostle Paul also experienced numerous hardships in his ministry, including persecution, imprisonment, and shipwrecks. Yet, he remained steadfast in his faith, declaring, "I can do all things through Christ who strengthens me" (Philippians 4:13).

These examples remind us that faith is not just about believing when everything is going well; it is about trusting God when the storms of life are raging. It is about holding onto His promises and believing that He is in control, even when we cannot see the way forward.

Faith is the foundation of the Christian walk. It is not just a belief or a feeling but an active trust in God and His promises. Men of faith throughout history have demonstrated what it means to trust in God's word, even in the face of trials and uncertainties.

As we embark on this journey of exploring the lives of these men of faith, let us remember that faith is not just a concept to be understood but a way of life to be lived out. Let us strive to be men of faith who trust in God's promises, persevere in the midst of trials, and demonstrate our belief through our actions. Let us hold fast to the confession of our hope without wavering, for He who promised is faithful (Hebrews 10:23).

Faith is a central theme in the Christian belief system. It is defined as the confidence in what we hope for and assurance about what we do not see (Hebrews 11:1). Faith is not just a feeling or a belief, but an active trust in God and His promises. In this first chapter of "Men of Faith", we will explore the question of what faith truly is and why it is essential for the Christian walk.

Defining Faith:

Many people have their own interpretations of what faith means. Some see it as blind trust or wishful thinking, while others view it as a logical decision based on evidence. However, in the context of Christianity, faith is much more profound. It goes beyond mere belief in the existence of God and extends to trusting His character and His promises.

Faith is not static; it is dynamic and requires action. James 2:17 tells us that faith without works is dead. In other words, faith should manifest itself in our actions and choices. It is not enough to say we have faith; we must demonstrate it through our deeds.

Another aspect of faith is persistence. Hebrews 11:6 states that without faith, it is impossible to please God, for whoever would draw near to Him must believe that He exists and that He rewards those who seek Him. This verse highlights the importance of continuing to trust God even when we cannot see the outcome. It requires perseverance and a willingness to wait on the Lord's timing.

Faith in God's Promises:

One of the central components of faith is trusting in God's promises. Throughout the Bible, we see examples of men and women who had unwavering faith in God's word. Abraham believed that God would fulfill His promise to make him the father of many nations, even when he and Sarah were well beyond childbearing age (Genesis 15:6).

Moses trusted that God would deliver the Israelites from slavery in Egypt, despite the many obstacles they faced along the way. David had faith that God would protect him from his enemies and establish his kingdom forever. These men of faith were not perfect, but they clung to God's promises and saw them fulfilled in their lives.

As Christians, we have access to the same promises that these men of faith did. We are told in 2 Peter 1:4 that through God's promises, we may become partakers of the divine nature. This means that we can have confidence in God's ability to transform us and fulfill His purposes in our lives.

Faith in the Face of Trials:

Another aspect of faith is trusting God even in the midst of trials and tribulations. Job is a prime example of someone who maintained his faith in God despite losing everything he had. He declared, "Though He slay me, yet will I trust Him" (Job 13:15).

The apostle Paul also experienced numerous hardships in his ministry, including persecution, imprisonment, and shipwrecks. Yet, he remained steadfast in his faith, declaring, "I can do all things through Christ who strengthens me" (Philippians 4:13).

These examples remind us that faith is not just about believing when everything is going well; it is about trusting God when the storms of life are raging. It is about holding onto His promises and believing that He is in control, even when we cannot see the way forward.

Faith is the foundation of the Christian walk. It is not just a belief or a feeling but an active trust in God and His promises. Men of faith throughout history have demonstrated what it means to trust in God's word, even in the face of trials and uncertainties.

As we embark on this journey of exploring the lives of these men of faith, let us remember that faith is not just a concept to be understood but a way of life to be lived out. Let us strive to be men of faith who trust in God's promises, persevere in the midst of trials, and demonstrate our belief through our actions. Let us hold fast to the confession of our hope without wavering, for He who promised is faithful (Hebrews 10:23).

In today's fast-paced and ever-changing world, the question of how to remain faithful to our Christian beliefs can seem like a daunting task. We are constantly bombarded with messages and influences that challenge our faith and push us to compromise our values. However, as men of faith, it is important to remember that our faith is not just a set of beliefs or practices, but a way of life. In this first chapter of "Men of Faith", we will explore how we can be faithful in today's world by anchoring ourselves in the Word of God, cultivating a deep relationship with Him, and staying connected to a community of believers.

The first step In being faithful in today's world is to anchor ourselves in the Word of God. In a world that is increasingly secular and hostile to Christian values, it is easy to become swayed by the opinions and attitudes of society. However, as men of faith, we must remember that our faith is built on a solid foundation – the truth of God's Word. The Bible is our roadmap for living a faithful life, and it contains wisdom and guidance for every situation we may face. By immersing ourselves in Scripture, meditating on its truths, and applying its principles to our lives, we can remain grounded in our faith and equipped to withstand the challenges of the world.

In addition to studying the Word of God, it is crucial for men of faith to cultivate a deep relationship with Him through prayer and communion. Prayer is our direct line of communication with God, and it is through prayer that we can draw near to Him, seek His guidance, and receive His strength. In today's fast-paced world, it is easy to prioritize other things over spending time with God, but as men of faith, we must make it a priority to seek Him daily, to listen to His voice, and to cultivate a heart of worship and gratitude.

Furthermore, staying connected to a community of believers is essential for remaining faithful in today's world. As men of faith, we are called to encourage and support one another, to bear each other's burdens, and to hold each other accountable in our walk with God. In a world that is increasingly individualistic and disconnected, the church provides a fellowship where we can find mutual support, encouragement, and accountability. By participating in a community of believers, we can strengthen our faith, grow in our relationship with God, and share in the joys and struggles of our Christian journey.

Being faithful in today's world is not easy, but as men of faith, we are called to stand firm in our beliefs, to trust in God's promises, and to live out our faith in a world that is often hostile to it. By anchoring ourselves in the Word of God, cultivating a deep relationship with Him, and staying connected to a community of believers, we can navigate the challenges of today's world with strength, courage, and unwavering faith. As we continue on this journey of faith, let us remember the words of Hebrews 11:1 – "Now faith is the substance of things hoped for, the evidence of things not seen." May we be men of faith who walk by faith, not by sight, and who trust in the promises of God in every season of life.

Finding Our Identity in Christ:

As men of faith, it is crucial for us to understand who we are in Christ and how this knowledge can strengthen our faith in Him. Our identity in Christ is not based on our past mistakes, our current struggles, or what others say about us. Instead, it is firmly rooted in the unwavering love and grace of God.

In the book of Ephesians, the apostle Paul writes to the believers in Ephesus, reminding them of their true identity in Christ. He tells them that they are chosen, adopted, redeemed, forgiven, and sealed with the Holy Spirit (Ephesians 1:3-14). This is a powerful truth that we, as men of faith, must also cling to.

When we understand that we are chosen by God, we can find confidence in the fact that He has a purpose for our lives. We are not here by accident or coincidence, but by divine appointment. This knowledge can give us the strength to face the challenges of life with boldness and courage, knowing that we are not alone.

As adopted sons of God, we are part of His family and have access to all the privileges and blessings that come with that relationship. We are no longer slaves to sin and fear, but sons of the Most High God. This truth should fill us with gratitude and humility, knowing that we have been grafted into the family of God through the sacrifice of Jesus Christ.

Through His blood, we have been redeemed and forgiven of all our sins. Our past no longer defines us, for we have been washed clean by the blood of the Lamb. This is a liberating truth that sets us free from the bondage of guilt and shame. We can now walk in the freedom and victory that Christ has won for us on the cross.

Furthermore, we have been sealed with the Holy Spirit, who is our guarantee of our inheritance in Christ. The Spirit dwells in us, guiding us, empowering us, and transforming us into the image of Christ. We are no longer slaves to our sinful nature, but sons of God who walk in the power and authority of the Holy Spirit.

When we understand and embrace our identity in Christ, we can then live out our faith with confidence and boldness. We can face the trials and tribulations of life with a sense of peace and assurance, knowing that we are secure in the hands of our Heavenly Father.

Our identity in Christ is not based on our performance or achievements, but on the finished work of Jesus Christ on the cross. It is a gift of grace that we must receive and walk in daily. When we align our thoughts, beliefs, and actions with the truth of who we are in Christ, we will find strength, courage, and perseverance to endure the storms of life.

As men of faith, let us hold fast to our identity in Christ, for it is the bedrock on which our faith is built. Let us meditate on the truths of Scripture that remind us of who we are in Christ, and let us walk in the fullness of our calling as sons of God. May our lives be a testimony to the transforming power of the gospel, as we live out our faith with conviction and boldness in a world that desperately needs to see the light of Christ shining through us.

Acting on Your Identity in Christ

Once you have found your identity in Christ, your life will never be the same. It is a transformative experience that leads you to act out of that new identity. No longer are you defined by the things of this world or by your past mistakes. Instead, you are a new creation in Christ, free to live out your faith in a way that reflects the love and grace of Jesus.

When you embrace your identity in Christ, you are called to become an imitator of Him. This means that everything you do should be a reflection of Jesus and His teachings. In the Bible, we are called to imitate Christ in his love for others, his compassion for the lost, and his unwavering faith in God. When we act in accordance with our identity in Christ, we are showing the world who we truly are and the love that we have received from our Savior.

One of the ways in which we can act on our identity in Christ is by living a life of integrity and honesty. As followers of Christ, we are called to be people of integrity who do not compromise our values or beliefs for the sake of personal gain. We should strive to be honest and trustworthy in all that we do, knowing that our actions speak louder than words. By living with integrity, we are able to show others the true character of Jesus and the transformative power of His love.

Another way in which we can act on our identity in Christ is by showing love and compassion to others. Jesus showed us what it means to love unconditionally and to show compassion to those in need. As His followers, we are called to do the same. This means reaching out to the marginalized, the oppressed, and the hurting, and showing them the love and grace of Jesus. By acting in love and compassion, we are able to show others the transformative power of Christ's love and the hope that it brings.

In addition to living a life of integrity and showing love and compassion to others, we are also called to live a life of faith and obedience. Faith is an integral part of our identity in Christ, as it is through faith that we are able to receive the grace and love of God. By living a life of faith, we are able to trust in God's plan for our lives and to obey His commands, knowing that He has our best interests at heart. When we act in faith and obedience, we are able to show others the power of God's love and the transformative impact that it can have on our lives.

As men of faith, we are called to act on our identity in Christ in every aspect of our lives. Whether it is in our relationships, our work, or our interactions with others, we should strive to be imitators of Christ and to reflect His love and grace in all that we do. By living a life of integrity, love, and faith, we are able to show others the transformative power of Christ's love and the hope that it brings. Let us, as men of faith, embrace our identity in Christ and act in a way that reflects His love and grace to the world around us.

Fulfilling Your Destiny as a Man of Faith:

As men of faith, we are called to walk in a way that is pleasing to God and to fulfill the destiny that He has set before us. This journey is not always easy, but with God by our side, we can run our race with integrity and perseverance.

1. Embrace Your Identity in Christ

Before we can fulfill our destiny as men of faith, we must first understand who we are in Christ. As believers, we are called sons of God and co-heirs with Christ (Romans 8:17). This means that we have been adopted into God's family and have all the rights and privileges of being His children.

When we embrace our identity in Christ, we can walk in confidence and boldness, knowing that we are loved and accepted by our Heavenly Father. This identity gives us the strength and courage to face any challenges that come our way, knowing that we are not alone.

2. Seek God's Will for Your Life

As men of faith, it is important that we seek God's will for our lives and align our plans and desires with His. Proverbs 16:9 tells us, "In their hearts humans plan their course, but the Lord establishes their steps." This means that while we may have our own plans and ambitions, ultimately it is God who directs our steps and leads us on the path He has for us.

To fulfill our destiny as men of faith, we must be willing to surrender our plans and desires to God and seek His will above all else. This may require us to step out of our comfort zone and trust God in areas where we may not have complete clarity. But when we seek His will and obey His leading, we can be confident that we are walking on the path to fulfilling our destiny.

3. Run Your Race with Integrity

In order to fulfill our destiny as men of faith, we must run our race with integrity. This means that we must live lives that are above reproach, seeking to honor God in all that we do. Hebrews 12:1-2 tells us, "Therefore, since we are surrounded by such a great cloud of witnesses, let us throw off everything that hinders and the sin that so easily entangles. And let us run with perseverance the race marked out for us, fixing our eyes on Jesus, the pioneer and perfecter of faith."

Running our race with integrity requires us to be honest, trustworthy, and accountable in all areas of our lives. It means living with a clear conscience, knowing that we are acting in a way that is pleasing to God. When we run our race with integrity, we can be confident that we are fulfilling our destiny as men of faith.

4. Persevere in the Face of Challenges

Fulfilling our destiny as men of faith will not always be easy. There will be times when we face challenges, setbacks, and obstacles that threaten to derail us from our path. But it is in these moments that our faith is tested and our perseverance is strengthened.

James 1:2-4 tells us, "Consider it pure joy, my brothers and sisters, whenever you face trials of many kinds, because you know that the testing of your faith produces perseverance. Let perseverance finish its work so that you may be mature and complete, not lacking anything." When we persevere in the face of challenges, we are strengthened in our faith and our character is refined, making us more like Christ.

As men of faith, we must be willing to endure hardship and persevere through trials, knowing that God is with us every step of the way. When we rely on His strength and trust in His promises, we can run our race with perseverance and fulfill the destiny that He has set before us.

Fulfilling our destiny as men of faith requires us to embrace our identity in Christ, seek God's will for our lives, run our race with integrity, and persevere in the face of challenges. When we align our lives with God's purposes and trust in His leading, we can confidently walk the path to fulfilling our destiny as men of faith. May we strive to honor God in all that we do and run our race with perseverance, knowing that He is with us every step of the way.

Chapter 2

Moses and His Faith in God

In the Bible, Moses is often remembered as one of the greatest leaders and prophets in Israelite history. His story is a testament to the power of faith in God, as he faced numerous challenges and obstacles throughout his life. Moses's journey from being a shepherd in Midian to leading the Israelites out of Egypt is a story of unwavering trust in God's plan.

Moses's faith in God was evident from the very beginning of his life. Born into a time when the Israelites were enslaved in Egypt, Moses's mother placed him in a basket and set him adrift in the Nile River, trusting in God's protection. Miraculously, Moses was found by Pharaoh's daughter and raised as a prince in the palace. Despite his privileged upbringing, Moses never forgot his roots and the plight of his people.

It was during his time In the palace that Moses's faith in God truly began to take shape. In Hebrews 11:24-27, we are told that Moses "chose to be mistreated along with the people of God rather than to enjoy the fleeting pleasures of sin." This decision to stand with his people against the oppression of the Egyptians was a clear demonstration of Moses's faith in God's justice and provision.

As Moses grew older, he became increasingly aware of his calling to lead the Israelites out of bondage. In Exodus 3, we read about Moses's encounter with God at the burning bush. Despite his initial reluctance and self-doubt, Moses trusted in God's promise to be with him every step of the way. This faith in God's presence and guidance gave Moses the confidence to confront Pharaoh and demand the release of the Israelites.

Throughout the Exodus story, we see Moses's faith in God tested time and time again. From the plagues that befell Egypt to the crossing of the Red Sea, Moses remained steadfast in his belief that God would deliver his people. In Exodus 14:13-14, Moses tells the Israelites, "Do not be afraid. Stand firm and you will see the deliverance the Lord will bring you today. The Lord will fight for you; you need only to be still."

Moses's faith in God was not without its moments of weakness. In Numbers 20, we read about the incident at Meribah where Moses struck the rock twice in anger instead of speaking to it as God had commanded. This act of disobedience cost Moses the chance to enter the

Promised Land. Despite this failure, Moses's unwavering trust in God's faithfulness remained a central part of his character.

In Deuteronomy 34, we see the culmination of Moses's life of faith as he stands on Mount Nebo overlooking the Promised Land. Despite knowing that he would not enter the land himself, Moses trusted in God's promise to fulfill the covenant with his people. In verse 10, we are told that "since then, there has not arisen in Israel a prophet like Moses, whom the Lord knew face to face."

Moses's story is a powerful reminder of the importance of faith in God's plan, even in the face of adversity and uncertainty. Like Moses, we are called to trust in God's presence, provision, and guidance as we navigate the challenges of life. As Hebrews 11:6 tells us, "And without faith it is impossible to please God, because anyone who comes to him must believe that he exists and that he rewards those who earnestly seek him."

Moses's faith in God serves as an inspiring example for all believers to follow. His willingness to trust in God's promises, even when faced with seemingly insurmountable obstacles, is a testament to the power of faith in God's plan. As we strive to walk in faith like

Moses, may we also be able to say with confidence, "The Lord will fight for us; we need only to be still."

In the Bible, Moses is often held up as one of the greatest examples of faith. From his miraculous birth to his leadership of the Israelites out of Egypt, Moses's life is a testament to the power of trusting in God. But sometimes it can be easy to look at figures like Moses and feel inadequate in our own faith. We may think that we could never measure up to someone like him, someone who heard the voice of God and spoke to Him face to face. But the truth is, we can have the same faith as Moses. We may not be perfect and may make mistakes, but God is there through all our struggles and desires the same closeness with us as He had with Moses.

Moses's life was not without its challenges. From the moment he was born, his life was in danger. Pharaoh had ordered all Hebrew baby boys to be killed, but Moses's mother hid him and eventually placed him in a basket in the Nile River where he was found by Pharaoh's daughter. Instead of being killed, Moses was raised in Pharaoh's household, but he never forgot his Hebrew roots. When he saw an Egyptian beating a Hebrew slave, he intervened and ended up killing the

Egyptian. Fearing for his life, Moses fled to the wilderness where he lived for many years.

It was during his time in the wilderness that Moses encountered God in a burning bush. God called Moses to lead the Israelites out of Egypt and promised to be with him every step of the way. Despite his doubts and fears, Moses trusted in God and followed His leading. Through plagues and miracles, Moses led the Israelites out of Egypt and towards the Promised Land.

Moses's faith was not without its struggles. He often questioned God's plan and doubted his own abilities. But through it all, God remained faithful. He provided for the Israelites in the wilderness, even when they grumbled and complained. He performed miracles to demonstrate His power and presence. And in moments of doubt, He reassured Moses of His love and guidance.

We may not be called to lead a nation out of slavery, but we are called to have the same faith as Moses. We are called to trust in God's plan for our lives, even when it seems impossible. We are called to seek His guidance and direction, even when we feel lost and alone. And we are called to rely on His strength and power, even when we are weak and weary.

Having the faith of Moses means having a deep and abiding trust in God. It means believing that He is with us in every situation, guiding us and providing for us. It means surrendering our fears and doubts to Him, knowing that He is always in control. It means seeking His will above our own, even when it requires sacrifice and obedience.

But how can we have the same faith as Moses? How can we overcome our doubts and fears and trust in God's plan for our lives? The key is to spend time in His presence, to seek His face and His will above all else. Just as Moses spent time in the presence of God on Mount Sinai, so too can we seek Him in prayer and in His Word. By drawing near to Him, we can experience His love and His guidance in a powerful and personal way.

We can also have the same faith as Moses by remembering God's faithfulness in our lives. Just as God performed miracles for the Israelites in the wilderness, so too has He performed miracles for us. He has provided for us in times of need, healed us in times of sickness, and comforted us in times of sorrow. By remembering His faithfulness in the past, we can trust in His faithfulness in the present and future.

We can have the same faith as Moses by stepping out in obedience to God's calling. Just as Moses had to leave his comfort zone and lead the Israelites out of Egypt, so too must we be willing to follow God's leading, even when it requires us to step out in faith. By obeying His commands and trusting in His plan, we can experience the same miracles and blessings that Moses did.

We can have the same faith as Moses. We may not be perfect and may make mistakes, but God is there through all our struggles and desires the same closeness with us as He had with Moses. By trusting in His plan, seeking His presence, and obeying His commands, we can experience the same faith and blessings that Moses did. So let us strive to have the faith of Moses, knowing that God is with us every step of the way.

The Parting of the Seas:

In the Bible, we read about the incredible story of Moses leading the Israelites out of slavery in Egypt. One of the most iconic moments in this story is when Moses parts the Red Sea, allowing the Israelites to escape their pursuers and continue on their journey to the promised land. This miraculous event was only made possible through faith – faith in God's power to deliver them, faith in His promises, and faith in His presence with them every step of the way.

Just like the Israelites, we too face seas in our lives that seem impossible to cross. Whether it be financial struggles, relationship problems, health challenges, or any other obstacle that feels insurmountable, we must remember that faith has the power to part the seas and make a way where there seems to be no way. Faith can truly move mountains and part the seas of our lives.

1. Faith in God's Power

The first step in parting the seas of our lives is having faith in God's power. Just as Moses trusted God to perform the miraculous and part the Red Sea, we must trust that God is capable of overcoming any obstacle we face. In Mark 10:27, Jesus says, "With man this is impossible, but not with God; all things are possible with God." This verse serves as a reminder that no matter how big the sea in front of us may seem, it is nothing compared to the power of our Almighty God.

When we face challenges that seem insurmountable, we must remember that God is not limited by our limitations. He is able to do exceedingly abundantly above all that we ask or think (Ephesians 3:20). By placing our faith in His power, we can trust that He will make a way for us where there seems to be no way.

Faith in God's Promises:

In addition to having faith in God's power, we must also have faith in His promises. Throughout the Bible, God makes countless promises to His people – promises of provision, protection, guidance, and deliverance. One of the most powerful promises we can hold onto is found in Romans 8:28, which says, "And we know that in all things God works for the

Faith in the Wilderness:

In life, we all experience times of uncertainty and difficulty. We face challenges that seem insurmountable and circumstances that leave us feeling lost and alone. In these moments, it can be easy to doubt whether God is truly with us, whether He is truly providing for us. But as men of faith, we know that our God is a God of miracles, a God who can make a way where there seems to be no way. It is in these wilderness moments that our faith is truly put to the test, and it is in these moments that we must hold fast to the promises of God.

The wilderness is a common motif in the Bible, symbolizing a period of testing and trial. It Is a place of desolation, where the usual comforts of life are stripped away and we are left with nothing but our faith in God. In the Old Testament, we see the Israelites wandering in the wilderness for 40 years, a period of testing and refinement before they could enter the promised land. In the New Testament, we see Jesus himself being led into the wilderness to be tempted by the devil, a time of testing before he began his ministry.

In our own lives, we may also find ourselves in the wilderness at times. It may be a period of financial difficulty, a season of illness, a time of relational turmoil. Whatever form it takes, the wilderness is a place where our faith is truly put to the test. It is easy to trust God when everything is going well, when our needs are met and our prayers are answered. But when we find ourselves in the wilderness, when our circumstances seem bleak and our prayers seem to go unanswered, it can be tempting to despair.

But as men of faith, we know that God is with us even in the wilderness. We know that He is a God who provides for His children, who cares for us in our time of need. In Psalm 23, we are reminded that even though we walk through the valley of the shadow of death, we do not need to fear, for God is with us. He is our shepherd, guiding us through the darkest times of our lives, providing us with everything we need.

In the wilderness, our faith is refined like gold in the fire. It is in these moments of trial that we truly learn to trust in God, to rely on His provision. In the wilderness, we learn that our God is a God of abundance, a God who can make streams flow in the desert and provide manna from heaven. Just as He provided for the Israelites in the wilderness, so too will He provide for us in our time of need.

But our faith in the wilderness is not just about trusting God to provide for our physical needs. It is also about trusting Him to provide for our spiritual needs. In the wilderness, we may feel spiritually dry and distant from God. We may struggle to hear His voice or feel His presence. But it is in these moments that we must cling to our faith, knowing that God is still with us, even when we cannot see or feel Him.

In the wilderness, we are called to draw near to God, to seek Him with all our hearts. It is in these moments of desperation that we learn to rely on God alone, to surrender our own strength and trust in His. It is in the wilderness that we are reminded of our utter dependence on God, of our need for His grace and mercy.

As men of faith, we must remember that the wilderness is not the end of our journey, but a necessary part of it. It is in the wilderness that we are molded and shaped into the men God has called us to be. It is in the wilderness that our faith is tested and refined, strengthened and deepened. And it is in the wilderness that we learn to trust in the God who provides for us, even in the darkest times of our lives.

So let us be men of faith in the wilderness, trusting in the God who never leaves us or forsakes us. Let us hold fast to the promises of God, knowing that He is with us always, even in the darkest moments of our lives. And let us remember that the wilderness is not the end of our story, but a stepping stone to greater faith and deeper intimacy with our Creator.

Chapter 3

Abraham – The Father of Faith

In this chapter of "Men of Faith," we will be exploring the life of Abraham, a man who is often referred to as the Father of Faith. His story is one of unwavering trust in God, even in the face of seemingly insurmountable challenges. Abraham's journey is a testament to the power of faith and serves as an inspiration to men of all ages.

Abraham's story begins in the book of Genesis, where we are introduced to him as Abram. He was a man of great wealth and stature, living in the city of Ur with his wife Sarai. However, despite his material wealth, Abram longed for something more. He sought a deeper relationship with God and desired to fulfill his purpose in life.

It was during this time that God called Abram to leave his homeland and go to a land that He would show him. This was no easy task, as it required Abram to leave behind everything he had ever known and step out in faith into the unknown. But Abram did not waver. He trusted in God's promise and set out on the journey with Sarai by his side.

As they traveled to the land of Canaan, Abram faced many trials and challenges. There were times when they encountered famine, opposition from neighboring tribes, and even doubts within their own hearts. But through it all, Abram remained steadfast in his faith. He believed in God's promise that he would become the father of a great nation, even though he and Sarai were already advanced in age and childless.

One of the most significant moments in Abram's journey of faith came when God made a covenant with him. In Genesis 15, God promised Abram that his descendants would be as numerous as the stars in the sky. And Abram believed the Lord, and He credited it to him as righteousness. This act of faith was a turning point in Abram's life. It was a moment of deep intimacy with God, where Abram's trust in Him was fully realized.

However, Abram's faith was put to the ultimate test when God asked him to sacrifice his only son, Isaac. This was a devastating request, as Isaac was the child of promise, the one through whom God's covenant with Abram would be fulfilled. But once again, Abram did not hesitate. He trusted in God's wisdom and faithfulness, believing that He would provide a way.

As Abram raised the knife to sacrifice Isaac, God intervened and provided a ram as a substitute. This was a powerful demonstration of Abram's faith and obedience. He was willing to surrender the most precious thing in his life because he trusted in God's plan. And because of his faith, God reaffirmed His covenant with Abram, promising to bless him and make his descendants as numerous as the stars in the sky.

Abraham's story is one of courage, perseverance, and unwavering faith. He is a shining example of what it means to trust in God completely, even when the circumstances seem impossible. Abraham's faith was not based on what he could see or understand but on the character of God. He believed that God was faithful to His promises and that He would fulfill them in His perfect timing.

As men of faith, we can learn valuable lessons from Abraham's life. We can be encouraged to trust God wholeheartedly, even when we face challenges and uncertainties. We can be inspired to step out in faith, knowing that God will guide us and provide for us along the way. And we can be reminded that true faith is not just believing in God's existence but trusting in His goodness and sovereignty.

Abraham's story is a powerful reminder that faith is not just a belief but a journey of obedience and trust. His life challenges us to deepen our relationship with God, to seek His will above all else, and to walk in faith even when the path is unclear. Let us strive to be men of faith like Abraham, who trust in God's promises and follow Him wholeheartedly.

Trusting in the Impossible:

In our journey of faith, there are times when the vision God has placed in our hearts seems impossible. We are faced with challenges, obstacles, and circumstances that make us question whether God's promises will ever come to fruition. In these moments, it is crucial for us to remember the story of Abraham, a man who exhibited unwavering faith in the face of impossibility.

Abraham's story is found in the book of Genesis, where God promises him descendants as numerous as the stars in the sky, even though he and his wife Sarah were well advanced in years and barren. Despite the seeming impossibility of the situation, Abraham chose to believe in God's promise. He trusted in the faithfulness and power of God, even when all circumstances pointed to the contrary.

Abraham's faith was not blind optimism or wishful thinking. It was rooted in a deep understanding of the character of God. He knew that God was faithful to His promises, even when they seemed too incredible to be true. Abraham's faith was a proactive choice to believe in what God had said, even when everything around him screamed otherwise.

As we navigate through our own journeys of faith, we can learn valuable lessons from Abraham's example. When faced with seemingly impossible situations, we can choose to trust in the faithfulness and power of God, just as Abraham did. Here are a few key principles to keep in mind when the vision seems impossible:

1. Remember God's Promises: Just as Abraham clung to God's promise of descendants, we must hold onto the promises God has given us. His word is a firm foundation that we can lean on, even when everything around us seems shaky. By immersing ourselves in Scripture and meditating on God's promises, we can find the strength and courage to press on in faith.

2. Walk by Faith, Not by Sight: It can be easy to rely on what we see with our physical eyes, but true faith requires us to trust in the unseen. When the vision seems impossible, we must choose to walk by faith, believing in the invisible hand of God working behind the scenes. As the apostle Paul reminds us in 2 Corinthians 5:7, "For we walk by faith, not by sight."

3. Seek God's Guidance: When we are unsure of how to proceed in the face of impossibility, we can turn to God for guidance. Just as Abraham sought God's direction in his journey, we can seek His wisdom through prayer, seeking counsel from godly mentors, and listening for His voice through His word. God is always ready to guide us if we are willing to listen and obey.

4. Embrace the Process: Abraham's journey of faith was not without its challenges and setbacks. There were times when he faltered and doubted, but he ultimately chose to trust in God's plan. In the same way, we must be willing to embrace the process of faith, knowing that God is refining us and preparing us for the fulfillment of His

promises. As we persevere through trials and difficulties, our faith will be strengthened and our character shaped.

5. Believe in the Power of God: When the vision seems impossible, we must remember that nothing is too difficult for God. He is able to do far more abundantly than all we ask or think (Ephesians 3:20). Our role is to trust in His power and sovereignty, knowing that He is able to bring about the impossible in His perfect timing and way.

As we reflect on Abraham's journey of faith, we are encouraged to trust in the impossible. No matter how daunting the vision may seem, we can have faith in the faithfulness and power of God. Just as Abraham's faith was credited to him as righteousness (Romans 4:3), so too can our faith be a pleasing offering to God. Let us press on in faith, believing that God is able to do immeasurably more than we could ever ask or imagine.

Embracing the Process of Faith:

In our journey of faith, we often find ourselves faced with challenges and obstacles that test our beliefs and trust in God. It is during these times that we must learn to embrace the process of faith, understanding that it is not always easy or straightforward. Just as a seed must be planted, watered, and nurtured before it can grow into a strong and fruitful tree, so too must our faith be cultivated and developed over time.

The Bible tells us that faith Is the substance of things hoped for, the evidence of things not seen (Hebrews 11:1). It is a confident assurance in what we do not yet see, trusting in God's promises and His plan for our lives. However, this type of faith does not come easily or instantly. It requires patience, perseverance, and a willingness to surrender control and trust in God's timing.

One of the key aspects of embracing the process of faith is learning to let go of our own preconceived notions and expectations. We must be willing to relinquish our desires for immediate answers and instant gratification, and instead, trust that God's timing is perfect and His plan is far greater than anything we could imagine. This requires a willingness to surrender our own will and submit to God's will, even when it may be difficult or uncomfortable.

Another important aspect of embracing the process of faith is learning to persevere through trials and tribulations. The Bible tells us that we will face various trials in this life, but we are called to count it all joy when we fall into various trials, knowing that the testing of our faith produces patience (James 1:2-3). It is through these challenges and struggles that our faith is refined and strengthened, as we learn to rely on God's strength and grace to sustain us through difficult times.

Furthermore, embracing the process of faith also involves seeking guidance and wisdom from God's Word and prayer. The Bible is filled with stories of men and women who faced impossible situations and insurmountable obstacles, yet through their unwavering faith and trust in God, they were able to overcome adversity and experience His miraculous provision and protection. By immersing ourselves in Scripture and spending time in prayer, we can draw closer to God and allow His Word to guide and sustain us through the ups and downs of life.

Finally, embracing the process of faith requires a willingness to step out in faith and take risks for the sake of the Gospel. The Bible is filled with examples of men and women who took bold and courageous steps of faith, trusting in God's provision and guidance to lead them to victory. Whether it was Abraham leaving his homeland to follow God's call, or David facing Goliath with nothing but a sling and a stone, these heroes of the faith were willing to take risks and trust in God's faithfulness to see them through.

Embracing the process of faith is an ongoing journey that requires patience, perseverance, and a willingness to surrender control and trust in God's plan. By letting go of our own expectations and desires, persevering through trials and tribulations, seeking guidance from God's Word and prayer, and taking risks for the sake of the Gospel, we can cultivate a deep and abiding faith that will sustain us through all the challenges and obstacles we face in life. May we all strive to be men and women of faith, trusting in God's promises and His plan for our lives, no matter how difficult or uncertain the path may seem.

Having Faith Like Abraham:

So how we can learn to have faith like him. Abraham, the father of faith, is a shining example of what it means to trust in God completely and wholeheartedly. His journey of faith is not only inspiring, but it also serves as a blueprint for our own walk with God.

Abraham's faith journey begins without hesitation, Abraham obeys God's command and embarks on a journey of faith that will ultimately lead him to become the father of many nations.

One of the key aspects of Abraham's faith is his unwavering trust in God's promises. Despite his advanced age and the impossibility of having a child with his wife Sarah, Abraham believes that God will fulfill His promise to make him a great nation. In Hebrews 11:11, we read that "By faith, even Sarah herself received ability to conceive, even beyond the proper time of life, since she considered Him faithful who had promised."

Like Abraham, we must learn to trust in God's promises, even when they seem impossible or unlikely. We may face obstacles and challenges along the way, but if we hold on to God's promises and trust in His faithfulness, we can be assured that He will fulfill His plans for us in His perfect timing.

Another important lesson we can learn from Abraham is his willingness to step out in faith and obey God, even when the path ahead is uncertain. In Genesis 22, we see Abraham's ultimate test of faith when God asks him to sacrifice his beloved son Isaac. Without hesitation, Abraham obeys God's command and demonstrates his unwavering trust in His sovereignty.

Abraham's obedience in the face of such a difficult trial is a testament to his deep faith and trust in God's wisdom and goodness. As Christians, we are called to follow Abraham's example and be willing to surrender our will to God's will, even when it may seem challenging or impossible.

Abraham's faith journey is a powerful reminder that true faith requires us to step out of our comfort zones and trust in God's leading, even when the path ahead is unclear. We may not always understand God's ways or His timing, but if we trust in His faithfulness and obey His commands, we can be confident that He will guide us and fulfill His purposes in our lives.

In James 2:23, we read that "Abraham believed God, and it was reckoned to him as righteousness." Like Abraham, we are called to believe in God and trust in His promises with unwavering faith. May we strive to emulate Abraham's example of faith and obedience, trusting in God's goodness and sovereignty as we journey through life's trials and challenges.

As we conclude this chapter on faith like Abraham, let us reflect on the words of Hebrews 11:6, which states that "Without faith, it is impossible to please Him, for he who comes to God must believe that He is and that He is a rewarder of those who seek Him." May we seek to cultivate a deep and abiding faith in God, trusting in His promises and obeying His commands with unwavering confidence in His faithfulness.

Chapter 4:

Imperfection doesn't mean unfaithful

Jacob, a prominent figure in the Bible, is known for his faith in God despite facing challenging circumstances. His story is a powerful example of how faith can sustain us through difficult times and lead us to a deeper relationship with God.

Jacob, whose name means "heel grabber" or "deceiver," was the son of Isaac and Rebekah, and the grandson of Abraham. From a young age, Jacob's life was marked by deception and manipulation. He tricked his brother Esau into giving up his birthright and later deceived his father Isaac into giving him the blessing meant for his older brother. Despite his flawed character, Jacob's story shows how God can work through imperfect people to accomplish his purposes.

One of the defining moments of Jacob's life was when he wrestled with God at Peniel. In Genesis 32:22-31, we read about how Jacob, on the eve of his reunion with Esau, wrestled with a mysterious man throughout the night. This encounter was a test of Jacob's faith and devotion to God. Despite being physically wounded, Jacob refused to let go until he received a blessing from God. In the end, God changed Jacob's name to Israel, signifying his new identity as a man who has wrestled with God and prevailed.

Jacob's faith was also tested through the trials and tribulations he faced in his life. From fleeing his brother Esau to facing Laban's deceit and manipulation, Jacob's faith was continually challenged. However, through it all, Jacob remained steadfast in his belief in God's promises. He trusted in God's faithfulness and provision, even when his circumstances seemed bleak.

One of the most inspiring aspects of Jacob's faith was his willingness to wait patiently for God's timing. After years of separation from his beloved son Joseph, Jacob never lost hope that God would reunite them. His faith was rewarded when Joseph was reunited with his family, and Jacob's heart was filled with joy and gratitude.

Jacob's story teaches us valuable lessons about faith and trust in God. Despite his flaws and mistakes, Jacob's unwavering faith in God's promises sustained him through life's trials. His story reminds us that God can work through our weaknesses and imperfections to accomplish his purposes.

As men of faith, we can learn from Jacob's example and strive to trust God's timing and plans for our lives. Like Jacob, we may face challenges and obstacles along the way, but we can take comfort in knowing that God is with us every step of the journey. Let us draw strength from Jacob's story and continue to walk in faith, believing that God will fulfill his promises in our lives.

Jacob's faith is a powerful example of how God can work in and through imperfect people to accomplish his purposes. His story serves as a reminder that faith is not about being perfect, but about trusting in God's faithfulness and provision. As men of faith, let us take inspiration from Jacob's life and continue to trust in God's promises, knowing that he is always with us, guiding us through life's challenges and triumphs.

Jacob's Imperfection and Faith in God

Jacob's journey is a powerful example of how God can use flawed individuals for his divine purposes.

Jacob's story begins in the book of Genesis, where we are introduced to his character as a cunning and deceitful man. From a young age, Jacob displayed a manipulative nature, as seen when he tricked his brother Esau into giving up his birthright for a bowl of stew. Jacob's deception continued when he, with the help of his mother Rebekah, deceived his father Isaac into blessing him instead of his older brother.

Despite his deceitful ways, God chose Jacob to be the recipient of the promise given to Abraham and Isaac. This shows that God's grace is not dependent on human merit or perfection, but on his sovereign will and purpose. Even in our imperfections, God can still work in and through us for his glory.

Jacob's imperfections eventually caught up with him when he had to flee from his brother Esau, who sought to kill him for his deceit. During his journey, Jacob had a profound encounter with God at Bethel, where he had a dream of a ladder reaching from earth to heaven with angels ascending and descending. In this dream, God reaffirmed the covenant he made with Abraham and Isaac, promising to bless Jacob and his descendants.

This encounter marked a turning point in Jacob's life, as he realized the error of his ways and sought to mend his relationship with God. He made a vow to serve God and declared that the Lord would be his God. Jacob's willingness to acknowledge his faults and seek reconciliation with God is a powerful lesson for all of us. We must humble ourselves before God, confess our sins, and turn from our wicked ways in order to experience true transformation and restoration.

Jacob's journey was not without its struggles, as he faced many challenges and trials along the way. One of the most significant events in Jacob's life was his wrestling match with God at Peniel. During this intense encounter, Jacob wrestled with God until daybreak, refusing to let go until he received a blessing. In the end, God touched Jacob's hip, leaving him with a limp as a reminder of his dependence on God.

This wrestling match symbolizes Jacob's struggle to surrender his will to God and trust in his providence. Despite his imperfections and struggles, Jacob's perseverance and faith in God ultimately led to his transformation. He was no longer known as Jacob, the deceitful supplanter, but as Israel, the one who struggles with God and prevails.

Jacob's story is a powerful reminder that God can use imperfect people for his divine purposes. His grace is sufficient to cover our sins and weaknesses, and his power is made perfect in our weakness. Like Jacob, we must be willing to confront our imperfections, wrestle with God, and surrender our will to his in order to experience true transformation and blessings.

As we reflect on Jacob's journey, let us be encouraged to trust in God's faithfulness and goodness, even in the midst of our imperfections and struggles. Let us be like Jacob, who despite his flaws, had the faith to believe in God's promises and see them fulfilled in his life. May we learn from Jacob's example and strive to live a life of faith and obedience to God, knowing that he is able to work all things together for our good.

Overcoming Imperfections and Walking in Faith

In our journey of faith, we inevitably come face to face with our own imperfections. We are flawed and human, prone to mistakes and shortcomings. We may stumble and fall, but it is in these moments of weakness that our faith is truly tested. How we respond to our imperfections will determine the depth of our relationship with God and our ability to walk in faith.

The Bible is filled with stories of imperfect men who overcame their flaws and walked in faith. Take for example Peter, who denied Jesus three times before the rooster crowed. Despite his betrayal, Peter went on to become one of the greatest apostles of Jesus, spreading the gospel to the ends of the earth. His faith was tested, but he overcame his imperfections and trusted in God's grace to lead him.

Likewise, Paul, formerly known as Saul, was a persecutor of the early Christians. He was zealous in his persecution, believing he was doing God's will. But on the road to Damascus, Paul encountered the risen Christ and his life was transformed. He overcame his past and became a powerful witness for the gospel, traveling to distant lands and enduring great hardships for the sake of spreading the good news.

These men of faith serve as examples to us that no matter how flawed we may be, God can still use us for his glory. We may have made mistakes in the past, we may struggle with sin and temptation, but through the power of Christ, we can overcome our imperfections and walk in faith.

But how do we overcome our imperfections and walk in faith? The first step is to acknowledge our weaknesses and shortcomings. We must be honest with ourselves and with God about our failings. We cannot hide our imperfections or pretend they don't exist. Instead, we must bring them to the light and ask God for forgiveness and strength to overcome them.

Secondly, we must rely on the grace of God to transform us. We cannot change ourselves through our own willpower or strength. Only through the power of the Holy Spirit can we be transformed into the image of Christ. We must surrender our imperfections to God and trust in his power to change us from the inside out.

Thirdly, we must walk in faith, trusting that God will guide us and provide for us every step of the way. We must have a deep and abiding faith in God's promises, knowing that he is faithful to fulfill his word. Even when we face trials and tribulations, we must hold fast to our faith and trust that God will work all things for our good.

Finally, we must surround ourselves with a community of believers who will encourage and support us in our journey of faith. We cannot walk this path alone; we need the fellowship and accountability of other believers to help us stay strong and grounded in our faith. Together, we can overcome our imperfections and walk in faith, supporting and lifting each other up along the way.

As men of faith, we are called to be vessels of God's love and grace in a broken and hurting world. We are imperfect vessels, but God can use us to bring hope and healing to those around us. By overcoming our imperfections and walking in faith, we can be light and salt in a dark and tasteless world, pointing others to the love and redemption found in Christ.

May we be like Peter and Paul, overcoming our imperfections and walking in faith, trusting in God's power to transform us and using our lives to bring glory to His name.

In life, we all face trials and challenges that test our faith. It's easy to have faith when everything is going well, but what truly defines our faith is how we respond in times of testing.

When our faith is tested, it can feel like we are being pushed to our limits. We may question God's plan for our lives and wonder why we are facing such hardship. But it is in these moments that our faith is truly put to the test.

In the Bible, we see numerous examples of men who faced great trials and challenges that tested their faith. Take, for example, the story of Job. Job was a righteous man who faced unimaginable loss and suffering. His faith was tested in ways that most of us can only imagine. Despite all that he went through, Job remained steadfast in his faith and never wavered in his belief in God.

Similarly, we see the story of Abraham. God asked Abraham to sacrifice his only son, Isaac, as a test of his faith. Abraham could have easily questioned God's command and refused to follow through. But instead, he showed incredible faith and trust in God, believing that God had a greater plan in store.

These stories serve as powerful reminders for us as men of faith. When we face trials and challenges that test our faith, we must remember to trust in God's plan and remain steadfast in our belief. It's easy to give in to doubt and fear when we are faced with difficult circumstances, but as men of faith, we must rely on God's strength and power to see us through.

In times of testing, it's important to turn to prayer and seek guidance from God. He is our rock and our fortress, and he will never abandon us in our time of need. By drawing closer to God through prayer and seeking his wisdom, we can find the strength and courage to face whatever challenges come our way.

It's also important to remember that trials and challenges are a part of God's plan for our lives. He uses these difficult times to refine us and strengthen our faith. Just as gold is purified in the fire, our faith is refined through testing. It is through these trials that our faith is deepened and our relationship with God is strengthened.

As men of faith, we must also remember to surround ourselves with a community of believers who can offer support and encouragement during difficult times. We were not meant to walk this journey alone, and having a strong support system of fellow believers can make all the difference when our faith is put to the test.

Ultimately, how we respond when our faith is tested is a reflection of our true character and conviction in God. As men of faith, let us strive to remain steadfast in our belief, trust in God's plan, and draw strength from our relationship with him. In doing so, we can navigate life's challenges with grace and courage, knowing that our faith will see us through.

Chapter 5

Faith as Our Foundation

In the Bible, Hebrews 11:1 tells us that "faith is the substance of things hoped for, the evidence of things not seen." This verse captures the essence of what it means to have faith as a Christian. Our faith is our foundation, the bedrock upon which we build our lives and navigate the challenges that come our way. In this chapter, we will explore the importance of faith as our foundation and how it shapes our Christian walk.

As men of faith, we are called to trust in God's promises and believe in His power to guide us through life's ups and downs. Our faith is not just a belief in something abstract or intangible; it is a deep conviction that God is real, that He loves us, and that He has a plan for our lives. When we anchor ourselves in this truth, we can face any obstacle with courage and confidence, knowing that God is with us every step of the way.

One of the key aspects of having faith as our foundation is trust. Trusting in God means surrendering control and placing our hope and confidence in His wisdom and goodness. It requires us to let go of our own desires and plans, and instead, put our faith in God's perfect will for our lives. This can be challenging, especially in times of uncertainty or difficulty, but when we choose to trust in God, we open ourselves up to His blessings and guidance.

Another important aspect of faith as our foundation is perseverance. The journey of faith is not always smooth sailing; there will be times when we face trials and tribulations that test our resolve. In these moments, it is crucial that we hold onto our faith with unwavering conviction, knowing that God is using these challenges to strengthen our faith and mold us into the men He has called us to be. As the apostle Paul writes in Romans 5:3-4, "Not only that, but we rejoice in our sufferings, knowing that suffering produces endurance, and endurance produces character, and character produces hope."

Faith as our foundation also empowers us to live out our Christian values and beliefs in a world that can often be hostile to our faith. It gives us the courage to stand firm in our convictions, even when it may be unpopular or challenging to do so. As men of faith, we are called to be shining lights in a dark world, to be examples of God's love and grace to those around us. When we live out our faith with authenticity and integrity, we show others the transformative power of a life lived in relationship with Jesus Christ.

Ultimately, faith as our foundation is what sustains us through the storms of life and gives us the strength to press forward in our Christian journey. It is the rock upon which we stand, the anchor that keeps us grounded in a world that is constantly shifting and changing. As men of faith, we need to hold fast to our belief in God's promises, trusting in His sovereignty and goodness, and allowing our faith to guide us in all that we do.

Faith as our foundation is not just a belief or an ideology; it is a lifeline that connects us to God and sustains us through life's challenges. It is the source of our hope, the catalyst for our perseverance, and the strength that enables us to live out our Christian values in a world that desperately needs to see the light of God's love. May we, as men of faith, continue to build our lives upon the foundation of faith, trusting in God's plan for our lives and allowing His Spirit to guide us every step of the way.

The Impact of Our Faith on Others

As men of faith, we should never underestimate the power of our beliefs and actions on those around us. Our faith is not meant to be isolated and individualistic, but rather a light that shines brightly for all to see. It is important to know how our faith can impact others in profound ways.

One of the key ways that our faith affects others is through our relationships. Our faith should be evident in the way we treat our family, friends, and colleagues. Our actions should reflect the love, compassion, and forgiveness that we have received from God. When people see us living out our faith in a tangible way, it can inspire and encourage them to also seek a relationship with God.

Our faith can also be a source of strength and support for those who are going through difficult times. When we share our own struggles and how our faith has sustained us, it can provide hope and comfort to those who are facing similar challenges. Our faith can be a beacon of light in the darkness, showing others that there is a way through the storm.

Furthermore, our faith can serve as a witness to those who do not yet know God. When we live out our faith with integrity and authenticity, it can be a powerful testimony to the reality of God's love and grace. People are more likely to be drawn to a faith that is genuine and lived out in real life, rather than just preached from a pulpit.

In addition, our faith can have a transformative effect on the world around us. When we seek to live out the values of the Kingdom of God – love, justice, mercy, and compassion – we can be agents of change in our communities and society. Our faith can inspire us to speak out against injustice, to advocate for the marginalized, and to work towards a more just and inclusive world.

However, we must also be aware that our faith can have negative consequences if it is not lived out in a way that is consistent with the teachings of Jesus. Hypocrisy, judgmentalism, and self-righteousness can all undermine the credibility of our faith and drive people away from God. We must strive to live out our faith with humility, grace, and a willingness to admit our own shortcomings.

The Impact of our faith on others can be profound and far-reaching. Our relationships, our witness, our support, and our actions all play a role in shaping the way that others perceive God and His Kingdom. As men of faith, let us strive to live out our beliefs in a way that brings glory to God and points others towards the hope and redemption that can be found in Him.

Our Faith as Proof

In a world where doubt and skepticism abound, it can be challenging to maintain a steadfast faith in God. We are constantly bombarded with questions and challenges to our beliefs, leaving us to wonder if our faith is truly grounded in truth. However, as men of faith, we must remember that our faith is not blind, but rather it is the proof that God is real and active in our lives.

The Bible tells us in Hebrews 11:1 that "faith is the substance of things hoped for, the evidence of things not seen." This verse reminds us that faith is not just a feeling or belief, but it is tangible evidence of the unseen realities of God's existence and his promises to us. Our faith serves as a testament to the reality of God's presence in our lives and his faithfulness to fulfill his word.

As men of faith, we are called to walk by faith and not by sight (2 Corinthians 5:7). This means that even when we cannot see the physical evidence of God's work in our lives, we can trust in His promises and rely on His faithfulness to see us through. Our faith is the proof that God is with us, guiding us, protecting us, and providing for us in ways that defy human understanding.

One of the greatest examples of faith in the Bible is the story of Abraham. God called Abraham to leave his home and go to a land that He would show him, promising to make him into a great nation. Despite not knowing where he was going, Abraham obeyed in faith and trusted in God's promises. As a result, God blessed him with a son in his old age, fulfilling his promise to make Abraham into a great nation.

Abraham's faith was the proof of God's faithfulness and power to fulfill His promises. Like Abraham, we are called to step out in faith and trust in God's promises, even when they seem impossible or out of reach. Our faith is the proof that God is faithful to fulfill His word, no matter how impossible it may seem to us.

Another example of faith in action is found in the story of the Israelites crossing the Red Sea. When they were trapped between the sea and the pursuing Egyptian army, God miraculously parted the waters and allowed them to cross on dry land. The Israelites had to trust in God's power and faithfulness to deliver them from their enemies, and their faith was the proof that God was with them and would protect them.

In our own lives, we may face seemingly insurmountable challenges and obstacles that threaten to overwhelm us. It is in these moments that our faith is tested, and we must choose to trust in God's promises and rely on His strength to see us through. Our faith is the proof that God is with us, fighting on our behalf, and working all things together for our good (Romans 8:28).

As men of faith, we must continually strengthen and nurture our faith through prayer, reading the Bible, and fellowship with other believers. These spiritual disciplines help us to deepen our relationship with God and grow in our trust and reliance on Him. Our faith is not meant to be stagnant or shallow but must be continually nourished and cultivated to withstand the trials and challenges of life.

Our faith is the proof that God is real and active in our lives. It is the evidence of the unseen realities of His existence and His faithfulness to fulfill His promises. As men of faith, we are called to walk by faith and trust in God's power and goodness, even when circumstances seem bleak. Let us hold fast to our faith, knowing that it is the proof that God is with us, guiding us, and working all things together for our good.

Chapter 6

Stepping out in Faith against the Worldly Culture

In today's society, it can be challenging to stand firm in your faith and live according to the principles laid out in God's Word. The world around us often promotes values and beliefs that are contrary to what is taught in the Bible. It takes courage and conviction to go against the flow and be a light in the darkness.

One man who exemplifies this kind of faith is Apostle Greg Locke of Mt. Juliet, Tennessee. Locke is the founder and lead pastor of Global Vision Bible Church, a thriving congregation that is known for its boldness in proclaiming the Gospel message. He has built a reputation for being unapologetically outspoken on issues such as abortion, marriage, and political correctness, despite facing criticism and opposition from those who disagree with his views.

Locke's journey to becoming a fearless voice for truth in a culture that often embraces moral relativism and cultural Marxism was marked by moments of doubt and uncertainty. Like many Christians, he struggled with questions of how to navigate the tension between standing up for his beliefs and being loving and compassionate towards those who held differing opinions.

But Locke's faith in God never wavered. He knew that he was called to be a voice for the voiceless, to speak up for those who could not speak for themselves, and to defend the truth of the Gospel in a world that was becoming increasingly hostile towards Christianity.

One of the pivotal moments in Locke's ministry came when he took a public stand against the transgender bathroom bill that was proposed in Tennessee. Despite facing backlash from the media and receiving death threats from those who opposed his stance, Locke remained steadfast in his convictions. He knew that he was called to speak out against the moral decay that was creeping into society, and he was not willing to compromise his beliefs for the sake of popularity or acceptance.

Locke's courage and boldness inspired others to stand up for what they believe in, even when it meant facing persecution or ridicule. His example showed them that it is possible to be a man of faith in a world that is hostile to the message of the Gospel, and that God will always provide the strength and courage needed to stand firm in the face of adversity.

As Locke continued to speak out against the evils of the world, his ministry grew and flourished. People from all walks of life were drawn to his message of hope and redemption, and many were inspired to recommit their lives to Christ. His church became a beacon of light in a dark world, shining the love and truth of Jesus Christ to all who would listen.

Today, Apostle Greg Locke's ministry continues to impact countless lives, both locally and globally. His unwavering faith and commitment to speaking the truth in love have made him a powerful voice for the Kingdom of God, and his example serves as a reminder to all believers that we are called to be salt and light in a world that is in desperate need of the Gospel message.

As we reflect on Locke's journey and the impact he has had on the world around him, may we be inspired to step out in faith against the worldly culture, knowing that God is always with us and will empower us to be courageous and bold witnesses for the truth. May we follow in Locke's footsteps, knowing that our faithfulness to God's Word will always lead to eternal rewards and blessings beyond measure.

The question rises then..."Can I Be Like Greg Locke?"

In today's society, it is not uncommon to look up to certain individuals as role models or sources of inspiration. We often admire people who possess qualities that we aspire to have ourselves. However, as Christians, it is important to remember that our ultimate role model should be Jesus Christ. He is the one we should strive to emulate in all aspects of our lives.

Apostle Greg Locke, Known for his bold and outspoken stance on various social and political issues, has made a name for himself as a man of faith who is unafraid to speak his mind. Many Christians look up to him as a fearless leader who is willing to stand up for what he believes in, no matter the cost.

But the question remains: can I be like Greg Locke? Is it possible for me to have that same level of faith and courage to stand against culture and speak out on controversial issues? The answer lies in understanding the difference between admiring someone and seeking to be like them.

In his teachings, Apostle Locke often emphasizes the importance of living a life that is pleasing to God. He encourages his followers to pursue holiness and righteousness, and to always put Christ first in their lives. While it is admirable to look up to Locke as a man of faith, it is crucial to remember that our ultimate goal should be to be like Christ.

As followers of Jesus, we are called to imitate His example in all that we do. This means loving our neighbors, showing compassion to the marginalized, and living lives that reflect the character of Christ. While Locke may serve as an inspiration to us, our true role model should always be Jesus.

That being said, there is no reason why we cannot strive to have the same kind of exemplary faith and courage that Locke exhibits. While we may not all be called to be as outspoken or controversial as he is, we can still be bold in our convictions and stand firm in our beliefs.

One of the key lessons that we can learn from Locke is the importance of standing up for what is right, even when it is unpopular. In a world that is increasingly hostile towards Christian values, it is crucial for us to be bold in our faith and unafraid to speak the truth.

Locke's example serves as a reminder that we should not be afraid to push back against the prevailing culture and stand up for biblical principles. While it may be difficult and risky to do so, we can take comfort in knowing that we are following in the footsteps of those who have gone before us and stood firm in their faith.

While it is admirable to look up to individuals like Greg Locke as men of faith and courage, our ultimate goal should always be to be like Christ. As we seek to follow in the footsteps of our Savior, may we also be inspired by the example of bold and courageous Christians like Locke. May we have the faith and courage to stand against culture and speak out on issues that matter, always striving to live lives that reflect the character of Christ.

Standing for the Truth

It can be easy to compromise our beliefs in order to fit in or be accepted by those around us. We are bombarded with messages that tell us that right and wrong are relative, and that we should just go with the flow and do what feels good. But as men of faith, we are called to stand firm in our beliefs and live out our faith with courage and conviction, even when it goes against the tide of popular opinion.

Standing for the truth means being willing to speak up and defend what we know to be right, even when it is unpopular or met with resistance. It requires courage and faith to stand up for what we believe in, knowing that we may face criticism, ridicule, or even persecution for our beliefs. But as men of faith, we are called to be bold and unashamed in our convictions, trusting in God to give us the strength and wisdom to stand firm in the face of opposition.

One of the greatest examples of standing for the truth in the Bible is found in the story of Shadrach, Meshach, and Abednego. These three men were faced with a choice to bow down and worship the golden statue that King Nebuchadnezzar had set up, or face being thrown into a fiery furnace. Despite the pressure and threats they faced, they refused to compromise their beliefs and stood firm in their faith, trusting in God to deliver them. And God did deliver them, miraculously saving them from the flames and showing His power to all who witnessed it.

Like Shadrach, Meshach, and Abednego, we must be willing to stand for the truth even when it is difficult or unpopular. We must be willing to stand up for our beliefs and values, even when it means facing ridicule or opposition from those around us. We must be willing to trust in God's strength and guidance, knowing that He will never leave us or forsake us.

Standing for the truth also means living out our faith in our daily lives, even when it means going against the cultural norm. It means being a light in the darkness, shining God's love and truth to those around us. It means being willing to speak up when we see injustice or wrongdoing, and to be a voice for the voiceless. It means being a man of integrity and character, reflecting the love and grace of God in all that we do.

In a culture that is increasingly hostile to Christian beliefs and values, it is more important than ever for men of faith to stand firm in their convictions and live out their faith with boldness and courage. We must be willing to speak the truth in love, even when it is difficult or uncomfortable. We must be willing to stand up for what we believe in, even when it means facing opposition or persecution.

As men of faith, we have a responsibility to be a shining example of God's love and truth in a world that is desperately in need of both. We must be willing to stand for the truth and in our faith, even when the culture doesn't approve. And we can take comfort in knowing that God is with us, empowering us to stand firm and live out our faith with courage and conviction.

Apostle locke is a prime modern example of Shadrach, Meshach and Abednego...He stood in the face of adversity and stood strong even when faced with persecution from the very government that was designed to protect us. This kind of Faith is possible and definitely attainable. Staying in the Word constantly and praying without ceasing is the way to obtain a Locke-down of your faith that the enemy cannot steal from you.

Chapter 7

A Patriot of Faith

In a time where the world seems to be spiraling into chaos and uncertainty, there are still men of faith who stand strong as beacons of hope and light. One such man is Pastor Ken Peters, the leader of the Patriot Church in Lenoir City, Tennessee. Pastor Ken is no stranger to adversity and challenges, but through it all, his unwavering faith in God has kept him strong and steadfast.

Born and raised in a Christian home, Pastor Ken's faith was instilled in him at an early age. He grew up attending church regularly and was actively involved in youth ministry. As he matured in his faith, he felt a calling to full-time ministry and pursued a degree in theology. After completing his studies, Pastor Ken began his journey as a pastor, serving in various churches across the country.

In 2019, Pastor Ken felt a stirring in his heart to start a new church that would not only preach the gospel but also stand up for Christian values and principles. Thus, the Patriot Church was born. The church quickly gained popularity among those who shared Pastor Ken's passion for faith and freedom.

However, Pastor Ken soon found himself facing intense scrutiny and backlash from critics who labeled him as a radical and extremist. Despite the attacks, Pastor Ken remained resolute in his mission to spread the truth of God's word and stand up for what he believed in.

One of the defining moments in Pastor Ken's journey of faith came during the height of the COVID-19 pandemic. As governments around the world imposed strict lockdowns and restrictions on churches, Pastor Ken made the bold decision to keep the doors of the Patriot Church open. He firmly believed that the church was an essential place for people to find hope and support during such trying times.

Despite facing threats of fines and legal action, Pastor Ken stood firm in his belief that God would protect his church and his congregation. Miraculously, the Patriot Church remained untouched, and not a single member fell ill with the virus.

Through it all, Pastor Ken's faith never wavered. He trusted in God's plan and provision, knowing that He would always be by his side. His unwavering faith was not only an inspiration to his congregation but to believers all around the world.

As Pastor Ken continues his journey as a man of faith, he remains steadfast in his commitment to spreading the gospel and standing up for Christian values. Despite the challenges and obstacles he faces, he knows that God is with him every step of the way.

Pastor Ken Peters is a true example of what it means to be a man of faith. His unwavering belief in God's power and goodness has guided him through the darkest of times and has inspired countless others to trust in the Lord. As we navigate through the uncertainties of life, let us look to Pastor Ken as a shining example of faith and courage. May we follow in his footsteps and never lose sight of the incredible power of God's love and grace.

A Voice for the Unborn

In a world filled with darkness and despair, there are few who are willing to stand up and speak out against the injustices that plague our society. Pastor Ken Peters is one of those few. With a heart full of compassion and a soul filled with faith, Pastor Ken Peters has dedicated his life to being a voice for the unborn, even in the face of great opposition and persecution.

It all began several years ago when Pastor Ken felt a calling from God to start a church near a local Planned Parenthood clinic. He knew that this would not be an easy task, as Planned Parenthood was a controversial organization that provided abortion services to women. But Pastor Ken knew that God had called him to be a voice for the voiceless, and he was willing to do whatever it took to stand up for the unborn.

From the moment Pastor Ken opened up the services at planned parenthood, he faced intense backlash from those who supported Planned Parenthood. Protesters gathered, shouting insults and slurs at him and his congregation. But Pastor Ken remained steadfast in his faith, knowing that God was with him every step of the way.

Despite the persecution, Pastor Ken continued to speak out against abortion and to offer support and resources to women facing unplanned pregnancies. He worked tirelessly to educate his congregation and his community about the sanctity of life and the value of every human being, born and unborn.

One of Pastor Ken's greatest victories came when he was able to convince broken women who had planned to have abortions to choose life instead. These women, who were facing difficult circumstances and overwhelming pressure to terminate their pregnancies, found hope and support at Pastor Ken's church. Through his love and compassion, Pastor Ken was able to save the lives of countless unborn children.

But Pastor Ken's work did not go unnoticed by those who opposed him. He received countless threats and hate mail, But Pastor Ken refused to be intimidated, knowing that God was on his side and that he was fighting for a righteous cause.

Despite the challenges and the dangers, Pastor Ken continued to be a voice for the unborn. He spoke out against the horrors of abortion and the lies of Planned Parenthood, and he never wavered in his commitment to protecting the sanctity of life.

Today, Pastor Ken's church continues to thrive, and his message of hope and redemption reaches far beyond the walls of his congregation. He has become a beacon of light in a dark world, a voice for the voiceless, and a champion for the unborn.

As we look to the future, let us all be inspired by the faith and courage of Pastor Ken Peters. Let us stand with him in the fight against abortion, and let us never shy away from speaking the truth and defending the innocent. May we all be men and women of faith, like Pastor Ken, who are willing to stand up for what is right, no matter the cost.

Faith in the Face of Persecution and Evil

In our walk of faith, we are bound to encounter moments of persecution and face the presence of evil. However, it is during these challenging times that our faith is truly tested and refined. As men of faith, we must cling relentlessly to our belief in God's power and goodness, even when the world around us seems to be falling apart.

Persecution has been a reality for Christians since the beginning of the church. The Apostle Paul himself experienced numerous instances of persecution and hardship for his faith. In 2 Timothy 3:12, he reminds us that "Indeed, all who desire to live a godly life in Christ

Jesus will be persecuted." This verse serves as a warning to us as men of faith that persecution is to be expected as we strive to live out our beliefs in a world that often opposes them.

When persecution comes our way, it can be easy to falter in our faith and question God's goodness. We may wonder why a loving God would allow us to suffer for our beliefs. However, it is during these moments of persecution that our faith is truly put to the test. Will we continue to trust in God's plan for our lives, even when it seems that the world is against us? Will we hold fast to our beliefs, even when it may cost us dearly?

One of the key aspects of maintaining faith in the face of persecution is to remember the examples of those who have gone before us. The Bible is filled with stories of men and women who faced intense persecution for their beliefs, yet remained steadfast in their faith. The story of Job, for example, serves as a powerful reminder that even in the midst of intense suffering, we can trust in God's goodness and plan for our lives.

In addition to drawing strength from the examples of those who have faced persecution before us, we must also rely on the power of prayer to sustain us during challenging times. Jesus himself modeled this for us in his own life, regularly retreating to pray and seek guidance from his heavenly Father. When we face persecution and evil, we must follow his example and spend time in prayer, seeking God's wisdom and strength to endure.

Another crucial aspect of maintaining faith in the face of persecution is to remember that God is ultimately in control. Even when it may seem like evil is prevailing in the world, we can take comfort in the knowledge that God is sovereign and will ultimately bring about justice and redemption. Romans 8:28 reminds us that "And we know that for those who love God all things work together for good, for those who are called according to his purpose." Even in the midst of persecution, we can trust that God is working all things together for our ultimate good.

As men of faith, we must also remember the importance of standing strong in the face of evil. The Bible warns us that "our struggle is not against flesh and blood, but against the rulers, against the authorities, against the powers of this dark world and against the spiritual forces of evil in the heavenly realms" (Ephesians 6:12). In a world that is often filled with darkness and evil, we are called to be lights, shining the truth and love of Christ in all that we do.

Standing strong against evil requires a firm foundation in our faith and an unwavering commitment to living out the principles of the gospel. We must be diligent in studying God's word and praying regularly, so that we may be equipped to resist the temptations and schemes of the enemy. Additionally, we must surround ourselves with a community of believers who can support and uplift us in times of trial.

Ultimately, having faith in the face of persecution and evil requires a deep trust in God's goodness, even when the circumstances around us seem bleak. We must hold fast to the promises of scripture and remember that God is faithful to guide and protect us in all situations. As men of faith, we are called to be beacons of light in a dark world, standing firm in our beliefs and trust in God's plan for our lives.

As we navigate the challenges of persecution and evil in our lives, may we always remember the words of Hebrews 11:1: "Now faith is confidence in what we hope for and assurance about what we do not see." Let us cling to our faith with unwavering confidence, knowing that God is with us always, even in the darkest of times. May we be men of faith who shine brightly in a world desperately in need of the light of Christ.

It's men like Pastor Ken Peters that give us inspiration knowing that God is not done. Faith is needed and it is the driving force for what we do while we are here on this earth. With the Holy Spirit and His guidance we can face anything that the devil throws our way.

Chapter 8

The Fruit of Faith

In the previous chapters of "Men of Faith," we have delved into what it means to have faith, how faith is cultivated, and the importance of standing firm in our faith during times of trial and tribulation. But now, in chapter 9, we will shift our focus to the fruit of faith. What is the evidence of faith in our lives? How does faith manifest itself in our words and actions?

The Apostle James, in his letter to the early Christians, writes, "Faith by itself, if it is not accompanied by action, is dead" (James 2:17). This verse serves as a powerful reminder that true faith is not merely a belief or a set of doctrines, but a living, active force that transforms our lives from the inside out. It is through our actions that our faith is made visible to the world.

One of the key fruits of faith is love. In his first letter to the Corinthians, the Apostle Paul writes, "And now these three remain: faith, hope and love. But the greatest of these is love" (1 Corinthians 13:13). Love is the hallmark of a true believer, for as Jesus himself said, "By this everyone will know that you are my disciples, if you love one another" (John 13:35). Our faith is made evident through our love for God and for our neighbors, as we seek to imitate the sacrificial love of Christ in all that we do.

Another fruit of faith is joy. In the book of Galatians, Paul lists joy as one of the fruits of the Spirit, alongside love, peace, patience, kindness, goodness, faithfulness, gentleness, and self-control (Galatians 5:22-23). This joy is not dependent on our circumstances, but is a deep-seated confidence in God's goodness and faithfulness, regardless of what may come our way. It is a joy that shines through even in the midst of suffering and trials, as we cling to the promises of God and trust in his ultimate plan for our lives.

Trust is another fruit of faith. In the book of Proverbs, we are exhorted to "Trust in the Lord with all your heart and lean not on your own understanding" (Proverbs 3:5). True faith requires a surrendering of our own plans and desires to the will of God, trusting that he knows what is best for us and will work all things together for our good (Romans 8:28). This trust is not blind or foolish, but is grounded in the unchanging character of God and his proven faithfulness throughout history.

Humility is yet another fruit of faith. In the book of Micah, we are told, "He has shown you, O mortal, what is good. And what does the Lord require of you? To act justly and to love mercy and to walk humbly with your God" (Micah 6:8). A true man of faith is marked by a humble recognition of his own weaknesses and shortcomings, and a willingness to submit to the leading of the Holy Spirit in all areas of his life. It is only through humility that we can truly experience the transformative power of faith in our lives.

The fruit of faith is evident in our love, joy, trust, and humility. It is a living, active force that transforms us from the inside out, making us more like Christ in all that we say and do. As men of faith, let us strive to bear fruit that is pleasing to God, that others may see our good works and give glory to our Father in heaven (Matthew 5:16). Let us be known not only for what we believe, but for how we live out our faith in the world, leaving a lasting impact for the kingdom of God.

Having Faith When We Don't Feel Like It

As men of faith, we often face challenges that test our resolve and commitment to God. There are times when we may feel overwhelmed, discouraged, or even disillusioned with our faith. In these moments, it can be easy to doubt, to question, and to waver in our belief in God's plan for us. However, it is in these very moments that our faith is truly tested and strengthened.

The Bible tells us in Hebrews 11:1 that faith is "the substance of things hoped for, the evidence of things not seen." It is the assurance that what we hope for will come to pass, even when we cannot see it with our own eyes. But what happens when we cannot seem to muster up that assurance? What happens when our faith feels weak and our hope begins to falter?

It is in these moments that we must remember that faith is not based on our feelings or emotions. It is a conscious choice that we make to trust in God, to believe in His promises, and to rely on His strength and guidance, even when we cannot see the way ahead. It is a decision to hold on to the hope that is within us, even when circumstances may seem bleak.

One of the greatest examples of having faith when we don't feel like it can be found in the story of Job. Job was a man who experienced great suffering and loss, yet he refused to curse God and turn away from his faith. Despite his friends' advice to abandon his beliefs, Job remained steadfast in his trust in God, declaring, "Though He slay me, yet will I trust in Him" (Job 13:15).

Like Job, we too must choose to trust in God's goodness and faithfulness, even when we face trials and tribulations. It is easy to have faith when everything is going well, but true faith is demonstrated when we continue to believe in God's promises, even when life is difficult. It is in these moments of testing that our faith is refined, deepened, and ultimately strengthened.

In 2 Corinthians 5:7, we are reminded to "walk by faith, not by sight." This means that we are called to trust in God's plan for us, even when we cannot see the outcome. It requires us to step out in faith, even when we do not feel like it, knowing that God is always with us, guiding us, and providing for us.

Having faith when we don't feel like it also requires us to seek God's presence through prayer, worship, and reading His Word. It is through these spiritual disciplines that we can find strength, encouragement, and hope to persevere in our faith journey. As men of faith, we must be intentional about nurturing our relationship with God, even when our feelings may not align with our beliefs.

Ultimately, having faith when we don't feel like it is a choice that we must make daily. It is a decision to trust in God's character, in His promises, and in His love for us, even when circumstances may seem overwhelming. It is a declaration of our reliance on God's grace and mercy, knowing that He is always faithful to fulfill His purposes in our lives.

So, let us be men of faith who choose to believe in God's goodness, even when we don't feel like it. Let us be men who walk by faith, not by sight, knowing that our trust in God will ultimately lead us to victory and triumph in Him. May we be reminded that faith is not based on our feelings, but on the unchanging truth of God's Word and His unfailing love for us.

The Choice of Faith

In our journey through the lives of men of faith, we have witnessed their unwavering trust and belief in God's promises. We have seen how their faith moved mountains, parted seas, and conquered armies. But behind every miracle, every triumph, lies a crucial decision – the choice to believe.

Faith is not a passive acceptance of what is, but an active decision to trust in the unseen and the unknown. It is a choice we make every day, in every circumstance, to believe that God is working all things for our good. The men of faith we have studied did not have all the answers, nor did they have all the details of how God would fulfill His promises. But they chose to trust anyway, knowing that God is faithful and true.

Abraham, the father of faith, faced the ultimate test of his faith when God asked him to sacrifice his son Isaac. Despite the seemingly impossible task, Abraham chose to trust God's plan, believing that He would provide a way out. And indeed, at the last moment, God provided a ram for the sacrifice, showing Abraham that his faith was not in vain.

Moses, another great man of faith, also faced a moment of choice when he stood before the Red Sea with the Egyptian army fast approaching. In that moment of fear and uncertainty, Moses chose to trust God's leading, raising his staff and parting the waters to deliver the Israelites from their enemies. It was a choice that required courage, faith, and obedience, but it was a choice that ultimately led to victory.

David, a man after God's own heart, faced many challenges throughout his life. From battling giants to fleeing from Saul's wrath, David's faith was tested time and time again. But in every trial, David chose to turn to God, seeking His guidance and strength. And in return, God raised him up as a mighty king, establishing His covenant with him and his descendants forever.

These men of faith teach us that the choice to believe is not always easy, but it is always worth it. It is a choice that requires humility, surrender, and persistence. It is a choice that may lead us into unknown territories, facing impossible odds, and enduring fiery trials. But in the end, it is a choice that leads to a deeper relationship with God, a greater understanding of His love, and a stronger confidence in His faithfulness.

As we look back on the lives of these men of faith, let us be inspired to make the same choice – the choice to believe. Let us choose faith over fear, trust over doubt, and hope over despair. Let us choose to walk in obedience, to seek God's will, and to follow His leading wherever it may take us. And in making this choice, may we experience the power of God's presence, the beauty of His promises, and the richness of His blessings.

The choice of faith Is a decision that shapes our lives, defines our destiny, and transforms our hearts. It is a choice that not only impacts us but also those around us, inspiring them to trust in God's goodness and grace. So let us continue to choose faith, to hold fast to our hope, and to run the race set before us with perseverance. And in doing so, may we become men and women of faith, standing firm in the promises of God and shining brightly as lights in a dark world.

Choosing Faith in Jesus

In our journey of faith, we face many decisions and challenges. One of the most important decisions we will ever make is choosing to have faith in Jesus. When we choose to follow Jesus, we are not just making a decision in the moment; we are making a decision that will impact every aspect of our lives now and for eternity.

Jesus said in John 14:6, "I am the way, the truth, and the life. No one comes to the Father except through me." This declaration is one of the most fundamental truths of the Christian faith. Jesus is not just a good teacher or a moral example; He is the Son of God, the Savior of the world, and the only way to God.

When we choose faith in Jesus, we are choosing to believe that He is who He says He is. We are choosing to accept His sacrifice on the cross as payment for our sins and to trust in His resurrection as victory over death. We are choosing to surrender our lives to His lordship and to walk in obedience to His commands.

Choosing faith in Jesus is not always easy. It can mean going against the grain of popular culture, facing persecution or ridicule from others, and making sacrifices that may be difficult or uncomfortable. But the rewards far outweigh the costs.

When we choose faith in Jesus, we are choosing to have a personal relationship with the Creator of the universe. We are choosing to experience His love, His grace, His peace, and His power in our lives. We are choosing to walk in purpose and destiny, knowing that our lives have eternal significance.

Choosing faith in Jesus also means choosing to live differently than the world around us. It means forgiving those who have wronged us, loving our enemies, serving the poor and needy, and standing up for justice and righteousness. It means living a life of integrity, honesty, and humility, reflecting the character of Christ to a watching world.

When we choose faith in Jesus, we are choosing to walk in freedom from sin and shame. We are choosing to receive forgiveness for our past mistakes and to be transformed by the renewing of our minds. We are choosing to let go of fear and anxiety, trusting in God's perfect love and sovereignty over our lives.

Choosing faith in Jesus is not a one-time decision; it is a daily commitment to follow Him wholeheartedly. It means spending time in prayer, in the Word, and in fellowship with other believers. It means seeking God's will in every decision we make and surrendering our plans and desires to His perfect purposes.

As men of faith, we are called to be bold and courageous in our stand for Christ. We are called to be leaders in our homes, our churches, and our communities, showing the world what it looks like to live a life fully surrendered to Jesus.

So today, I encourage you to choose faith in Jesus. Choose to believe in His love and His power to transform your life. Choose to walk in obedience to His

Word and to trust in His promises. Choose to make Him the center of your life and to follow Him with all of your heart, soul, mind, and strength.

As you do, you will experience the abundant life that Jesus promised to those who believe in Him. You will walk in victory over sin and death, knowing that nothing can separate you from the love of God. You will be a shining light in a dark world, pointing others to the life-changing power of faith in Jesus.

May this chapter inspire you to choose faith in Jesus today and every day, knowing that He is faithful and true, and that He will never leave you or forsake you. May you be a man of faith, walking in the footsteps of our Savior, and spreading His love and truth to all who cross your path. Amen.

Chapter 9

Supernatural Faith

In the journey of faith, there comes a point where our belief in God transcends the natural realm and reaches into the supernatural. This is when we move beyond simply trusting in what we can see and understand to trusting in the power and promises of God that defy human logic and reasoning. It is in this realm of supernatural faith that men of faith truly find their strength and witness the miraculous works of God in their lives.

The Bible is filled with examples of men who walked in supernatural faith and saw God move in incredible ways. From Abraham, who believed in God's promise of a son in his old age, to Moses, who led the Israelites through the Red Sea on dry land, to Peter, who walked on water towards Jesus – these men trusted in the supernatural power of God and saw extraordinary things happen.

One of the key elements of supernatural faith is a deep conviction in the character and nature of God. When we truly believe that God is all-powerful, all-knowing, and always faithful to His promises, we can trust Him to do the impossible in our lives. This kind of faith requires us to let go of our own limitations and doubts and fully surrender to God's will and purpose for our lives.

Another aspect of supernatural faith is the ability to see beyond the present circumstances and focus on the unseen realities of God's kingdom. In Hebrews 11:1, it says, "Now faith is substance of things hoped for and evidence of things unseen." This kind of faith enables us to trust in God's wisdom and timing, even when things seem impossible or hopeless in the natural realm.

Men of faith who walk in supernatural faith are not swayed by fear or doubt, but stand firm in their belief in God's power to overcome any obstacle. They are willing to step out in faith, even when it seems risky or illogical, knowing that God is always faithful to His promises. This kind of bold and unwavering faith is what sets men apart and allows them to experience the fullness of God's blessings and provision in their lives.

One of the greatest examples of supernatural faith in the Bible is found in the story of Shadrach, Meshach, and Abednego in the book of Daniel. When faced with the choice of bowing down to a false idol or facing certain death in a fiery furnace, these three men chose to trust in God's supernatural power to deliver them. Their words in Daniel 3:17-18 are a powerful testimony of their faith: "If we are thrown into the blazing furnace, the God we serve is able to deliver us from it, and he will deliver us from Your Majesty's hand. But even if he does not, we want you to know, Your Majesty, that we will not serve your gods or worship the image of gold you have set up."

The outcome of this Incredible display of faith was nothing short of miraculous. Not only were Shadrach, Meshach, and Abednego spared from the fiery furnace, but they also witnessed the presence of a fourth man in the fire who was none other than the Son of God Himself. This story serves as a powerful reminder that when we trust in God's supernatural power, He will always be with us in the midst of our trials and deliver us from harm.

As men of faith, we are called to walk in supernatural faith and believe in the impossible. This kind of faith requires us to fully surrender to God's will, trust in His character and promises, and step out in boldness and courage, even when it seems risky or illogical. When we trust in God's supernatural power, we can be confident that He will always be faithful to His word and work all things together for our good.

Let us be men of faith who walk in supernatural faith, trusting in the power of God to do the impossible in our lives. May we never waver in our belief in His promises and always stand firm in the face of trials and challenges, knowing that He is with us every step of the way. With supernatural faith, we can overcome any obstacle and witness the miraculous works of God in our lives.

Mountain Moving Faith

This type of faith is the kind of faith that believes in the impossible, that trusts in God's power to overcome any obstacle, no matter how big or insurmountable it may seem. It is the kind of faith that moves mountains, that brings about miracles and demonstrates the power and greatness of our Almighty God.

In the Bible, Jesus speaks about this kind of faith in Matthew 17:20, when he tells his disciples, "Truly I tell you, if you have faith as small as a mustard seed, you can say to this mountain, 'Move from here to there,' and it will move. Nothing will be impossible for you." Jesus is teaching his disciples that even a small amount of faith can be powerful enough to move mountains, to overcome obstacles, to bring about miracles.

One example of mountain moving faith in the Bible is found in the story of David and Goliath. In 1 Samuel 17, we read about how David, a young shepherd boy, faced the giant Goliath, a fierce warrior who was feared by all. Despite the odds being against him, David trusted in God's power to deliver him, and he stepped out in faith to face Goliath with just a sling and a few stones. And with that mountain moving faith, David defeated the giant and became a hero of the Israelites.

Another example of mountain moving faith is found in the story of the Israelites crossing the Red Sea. In Exodus 14, we read about how the Israelites were trapped between the Pharaoh's army and the Red Sea, with seemingly no way out. But Moses, their leader, trusted in God's power to deliver them, and he raised his staff and parted the waters of the Red Sea, allowing the Israelites to cross on dry land. With that mountain moving faith, the Israelites were saved from their enemies and delivered to safety.

These stories from the Bible are not just historical accounts, but they are also powerful examples of the kind of faith that God calls us to have. Mountain moving faith is a faith that believes in God's promises, that trusts in his power, and that is willing to step out in obedience and take risks for the sake of the Kingdom. It is a faith that does not shrink back in the face of obstacles, but that stands firm and declares, "Nothing is impossible for God."

But how do we cultivate mountain moving faith in our own lives? How do we grow in our faith and trust in God's power to overcome the mountains that stand in our way? Here are a few key principles to help us develop mountain moving faith:

1. Trust in God's promises – The first step to cultivating mountain moving faith is to trust in God's promises. The Bible is full of promises from God that tell us of his love, his power, and his faithfulness to us. When we meditate on these promises and believe them in our hearts, our faith is strengthened, and we are able to face any obstacle with confidence.

2. Pray with faith – Prayer is a powerful tool in cultivating mountain moving faith. When we pray with faith, believing that God can do the impossible, our prayers are filled with power and authority. Jesus tells us in Mark 11:24, "Therefore

I tell you, whatever you ask for in prayer, believe that you have received it, and it will be yours." When we pray with faith, mountains can be moved, and miracles can happen.

3. Step out in obedience – Mountain moving faith requires us to step out in obedience and take risks for the sake of the Kingdom. Just as David faced Goliath and Moses parted the Red Sea, we are called to step out in faith and trust in God's power to overcome the obstacles in our lives. When we are obedient to God's leading, he will enable us to do the impossible and bring about miracles in our midst.

4. Be persistent – Finally, mountain moving faith requires persistence and perseverance. Like the persistent widow in Luke 18 who kept coming to the judge until he granted her justice, we are called to persist in our prayers, our faith, and our obedience, even when the mountains in our lives seem insurmountable. When we persevere in faith, God will show himself faithful and bring about breakthroughs and victories in our lives.

Mountain moving faith is the kind of faith that believes in the impossible, that trusts in God's power to overcome any obstacle, and that is willing to step out in obedience and take risks for the sake of the Kingdom. It is a faith that moves mountains, that brings about miracles, and that demonstrates the power and greatness of our Almighty God. May we all cultivate mountain moving faith in our lives and be witnesses to the amazing things that God can do when we trust in him wholeheartedly.

Dead Raising Faith

In the world of Christianity, one of the most controversial and yet awe-inspiring aspects of faith is the belief in the power to raise the dead. Throughout history, there have been accounts of individuals who have displayed incredible faith and seen miraculous results in the form of raising the dead back to life. Let's explore the concept of dead raising faith and discuss how men of faith throughout the ages have demonstrated this remarkable power.

The Idea of raising the dead may seem far-fetched to some, but for those who believe in the power of God and the authority of Jesus Christ, nothing is impossible.

In the Bible, there are several instances where individuals were brought back to life through the power of God. One of the most notable accounts is found in the book of John, where Jesus raises Lazarus from the dead after he had been in the tomb for four days. This miraculous event not only demonstrated Jesus' power over death but also solidified the belief that with faith, all things are possible.

In modern times, there have been numerous reports of individuals who have been raised from the dead through prayer and faith. One such example is the story of Smith Wigglesworth, a renowned British evangelist and healer who was known for his incredible faith and miraculous healing ministry. On one occasion, Wigglesworth was called to pray for a man who had died suddenly. With unwavering faith, Wigglesworth prayed fervently and commanded the man to come back to life. To the amazement of all who were present, the man rose from the dead, completely healed and restored.

Another well-known example of dead raising faith is the story of George Mueller, a 19th-century Christian evangelist and orphanage director. Mueller was faced with a situation where one of the children in his care had passed away unexpectedly. Instead of accepting defeat, Mueller turned to prayer and faith, believing that

God could and would bring the child back to life. After hours of fervent prayer, the child miraculously came back to life, much to the awe and wonder of all who witnessed the event.

What sets these men apart is their unwavering faith in the power of God to overcome even the most impossible situations. They were not swayed by doubt or fear, but instead stood firm in their belief that God was able to do exceedingly abundantly above all they could ask or think. Their faith was not based on their own abilities or strength, but on the promises and power of God.

So how can we as modern-day Christians cultivate and strengthen our own dead raising faith? The key lies in a deep and intimate relationship with God, a lifestyle of prayer and fasting, and a commitment to studying and meditating on God's Word. Faith is like a muscle that needs to be exercised and strengthened regularly in order to grow and mature. By spending time in the presence of God, seeking His face, and aligning our will with His, we can tap into the same supernatural power that enabled men like Smith Wigglesworth and George Mueller to raise the dead.

It is important to note that not everyone will be called to raise the dead In the literal sense, but we are all called to walk in the same level of faith and dependency on God. Whether it be raising the dead to life or speaking life into dead situations in our own lives, dead raising faith is a powerful weapon in the arsenal of every believer. As we continue to press into God and seek His face, may we be like the men of faith who have gone before us, walking in the miraculous and supernatural power of the Holy Spirit.

Dead raising faith is not just a concept or theory, but a reality that can be experienced and lived out in our everyday lives. By studying the lives of men of faith who have gone before us, we can glean valuable insights and principles that will help us cultivate and strengthen our own faith. Let us be men of faith who believe in the power of God to perform miracles and raise the dead, knowing that with Him, all things are possible.

Chapter 10

Battle Ready Faith

In this chapter, we will explore what it means to have battle ready faith as men of faith in the Christian walk. The Bible speaks of a spiritual battle that we are all engaged in, a battle that requires us to be prepared and equipped with the armor of God. As men of faith, we must have a firm foundation in the Word of God and be ready to stand firm in the face of adversity.

The Apostle Paul tells us in Ephesians 6:10-18, "Finally, be strong in the Lord and in his mighty power. Put on the full armor of God so that you can take your stand against the devil's schemes... Stand firm then, with the belt of truth buckled around your waist, with the breastplate of righteousness in place, and with your feet fitted with the readiness that comes from the gospel of peace. In addition to all this, take up the shield of faith, with which you can extinguish all the flaming arrows of the evil one. Take the helmet of salvation and the sword of the Spirit, which is the word of God."

To be battle ready, we must first understand the reality of the spiritual battle that we are in. The Bible tells us that our struggle is not against flesh and blood, but against the spiritual forces of evil in the heavenly realms (Ephesians 6:12). This battle is not physical but spiritual, and it requires spiritual weapons to fight against the enemy.

One of the most important weapons in our arsenal is faith. Hebrews 11:1 defines faith as the substance of things hoped for, the evidence of things unseen. Faith is our trust and confidence in God and His promises, even when we cannot see the outcome. It is the substance of things hoped for and the evidence of things not seen.

As men of faith, we must have a faith that is unwavering, unshakable, and unmovable. We must have a faith that is not based on our circumstances or feelings but on the promises of God. We must believe that God is faithful and that He will do what He says He will do.

To be battle ready, we must also have a faith that is activated and put into action. James 2:14-26 tells us that faith without works is dead. Our faith must be demonstrated through our actions and obedience to God's Word. We must be doers of the word and not just hearers only.

In the midst of the battle, we must hold on to our faith and trust in God's sovereignty. We must remember that God is in control and that He has already won the victory. We must not be afraid or discouraged but have faith that God will fight for us and that He will deliver us from our enemies.

As men of faith, we must also be prayer warriors. Ephesians 6:18 tells us to pray in the Spirit on all occasions with all kinds of prayers and requests. Prayer is our communication with God, and it is through prayer that we can access the power of God to overcome the enemy.

As men of faith, we must be battle ready. We must put on the full armor of God and stand firm in our faith. We must be prepared for the spiritual battle that we are in and be equipped with the weapons of our warfare. We must have a faith that is unshakable, unwavering, and unmovable. We must believe in the promises of God and trust in His sovereignty. We must be prayer warriors and seek God's guidance and strength in the midst of the battle. With battle ready faith, we can overcome every obstacle and every enemy that comes against us.

The Shield of Faith

The shield of faith is an essential tool that every believer must utilize in their walk with God. It is a powerful piece of the armor that can protect us from the fiery darts of the enemy and enable us to stand firm in our faith.

The Bible tells us in Ephesians 6:16 to take up the shield of faith, with which we can extinguish all the flaming arrows of the evil one. This imagery of a shield is especially fitting when we consider the purpose and function of a shield in battle. Shields were used by soldiers in ancient times to protect themselves from incoming attacks and to deflect blows from their enemies. In the same way, our faith serves as a shield that guards us against the attacks of the enemy.

So, what exactly is the shield of faith? Faith is the confident belief in the promises and character of God. It is the assurance of things hoped for and the conviction of things not seen (Hebrews 11:1). When we have faith in God, we trust in His goodness, His power, and His faithfulness to fulfill His promises to us. This faith empowers us to overcome the trials and tribulations of life and to walk in victory.

But faith is not just a passive belief. It is an active response to God's word and His leading in our lives. Just as a soldier must raise his shield to block incoming attacks, we must actively engage our faith to shield ourselves from the schemes of the enemy. We must hold firm to the truth of God's word, even when circumstances seem bleak. We must trust in His promises, even when our emotions tell us otherwise. We must stand firm in our faith, knowing that God is always with us and will never leave us nor forsake us.

One of the key ways that we can use the shield of faith in our lives is by speaking God's word over our circumstances. The Bible tells us that the power of life and death are in the tongue (Proverbs 18:21). When we speak God's promises and truths out loud, we are declaring our faith and trust in Him. This act of faith not only strengthens our own belief but also releases the power of God into our situations. As we speak faith-filled words, we are erecting a shield of protection around us that repels the attacks of the enemy.

Another way that we can activate the shield of faith is by remembering God's faithfulness in the past. Just as David recalled how God had delivered him from the paw of the lion and the bear when facing Goliath (1 Samuel 17:34-37), we too can look back on our own lives and see how God has been faithful to us. Remembering God's past faithfulness helps to build our confidence in Him and strengthens our shield of faith.

The shield of faith Is a powerful tool that every believer has at their disposal. It is a shield that can protect us from the fiery darts of the enemy and enable us to stand firm in our faith. By actively engaging our faith, speaking God's word, and remembering His faithfulness, we can strengthen our shield and walk in victory. Let us take up the shield of faith and trust in God's promises, knowing that He is always with us and will never leave us nor forsake us.

In the book of Judges in the Bible, we see the story of a man named Gideon who was called by God to lead the Israelites against their enemies, the Midianites. Gideon was not a warrior by nature, he was a simple farmer. But God saw something in Gideon that he didn't see in himself. God saw a man of faith, a man who had the potential to do great things for his people.

In chapter 6 of the book of Judges, we see how Gideon was called by God to lead the Israelites. God appeared to Gideon and said to him, "The Lord is with you, mighty warrior." Gideon was taken aback by this statement, as he saw himself as anything but a mighty warrior. He questioned God, asking how he could lead the Israelites when he was the least in his family and from the weakest clan in Israel.

But God assured Gideon that he would be with him and that he would help him to overcome the Midianites. God asked Gideon to tear down the altars of the false gods in his land and to build an altar to the Lord. Gideon did as God commanded, and the people of Israel began to follow him.

In chapter 7 of the book of Judges, we see how God instructed Gideon to gather an army to fight against the Midianites. Gideon initially gathered 32,000 men, but God told him that the army was too large. God wanted to show the Israelites that it was not their strength or numbers that would win the battle, but their faith in him.

God told Gideon to send home all those who were afraid. 22,000 men left, leaving only 10,000. But God still felt that the army was too large. He instructed Gideon to take the remaining men to the water to drink and to watch how they drank. Those who lapped up the water with their hands were to be set aside, while those who knelt down to drink were to be sent home. Only 300 men remained.

Gideon was now left with only 300 men to fight against the vast army of the Midianites. But Gideon had faith that God would deliver them. He divided the 300 men into three groups and gave each man a trumpet and an empty jar with a torch inside. They surrounded the camp of the Midianites at night and at Gideon's signal, they blew their trumpets, broke their jars, and shouted, "A sword for the Lord and for Gideon!"

The Midianites were thrown into a panic and turned on each other. They fled in fear, and the Israelites pursued them and won a great victory. The battle was won not by the strength of the Israelites, but by their faith in God.

The story of Gideon teaches us that it doesn't matter how big the odds are against us. As long as we have faith in God, we can overcome any enemy or obstacle in our path. Gideon was just a simple farmer, but God saw his potential and used him to do great things. We too have the potential to do great things if we put our faith in God and trust in his strength and power.

As men of faith, we must remember that our battles are not fought by our own might or power, but by the Spirit of God within us. We must trust in God's plan for our lives and have faith that he will lead us to victory. Just as Gideon won the battle with only 300 soldiers, we too can overcome any enemy that stands in our way, as long as we have faith in God.

Chapter 11

Faith when integrity is compromised.

Another man of faith I want to point out is also a good friend. This man continues to show exemplary faith in his daily spiritual walk.

In the midst of a nation grappling with the aftermath of a devastating pandemic, Pastor Bryan Davis found himself entrusted with what felt like a divine opportunity: to serve as pastor of a quaint, traditional church nestled in the North Georgia Appalachian Mountains, mere months before the virus struck. This church, however, was already in turmoil due to the overbearing authority wielded by its last elder, worsened by his predecessor's complacency. Unlike him, He was determined to lead with conviction rather than mere compliance.

Over the next two and a half years, Pastor Davis' journey was a testament to surrendering to God's will and fervently praying for revival among the congregation, predominantly comprised of older retirees whom he felt deeply responsible to safeguard. During this time, they were blessed to host renowned figures such as DR. Ron

Phillips, Pastor Lindell Cooley, Bishop C. David Amos, Sister Donna Schambach, and Apostle Greg Locke, among other respected revivalists. Their visits, often undertaken without financial demands, were a stark contrast to the penny-pinching of the elder and his wife.

As the spiritual fervor grew, so did opposition. Behind the scenes individuals spent months attempting to extinguish the fire that God had ignited in his heart. Amidst this struggle, Pastor Davis received a stark warning from trusted friends—Apostle Marvin Booth, Tom Scarrella, and John James(former Lead Singer of "The NewsBoys"—foretelling a conspiracy against him and the impending end of his tenure.

True to their prediction, the elder and his wife escalated their machinations by involving higher authorities and manipulating circumstances to their advantage. Their efforts were bolstered by the appointment of a new presbyter who sought to usurp not only his leadership but also the church building itself. The climax came one rainy January morning when he was unceremoniously dismissed under false pretenses, presented with a choice that would define his integrity forever.

The then "Assistant Superintendent" told him "You are to preach Sunday .. afterward you will announce that it is your idea to leave the church and the next Sunday, you will have photo ops with all the people and pretend that you are happy. If not, I will cancel your severance pay and ban you for life from church property. No one can know the truth of this conversation " he grinned. They might leave if they learn the truth... you wouldn't wanna hurt the church... Would you?"

Faced with a demand to deceive his congregation about the circumstances of his departure, Pastor Davis found himself at a crossroads—a Martin Luther moment, as he would come to see it. Refusing to compromise his principles, cost him. He rejected their proposal despite the financial consequences and the banishment from church property that followed.

In the aftermath, guided by prayer and counsel from respected mentors, He stood firm. Integrity, he realized, was priceless. Despite losing severance pay and facing expulsion, he held onto the truth. Months later, Apostle Greg Locke affirmed his resolve by commissioning him as a pastor for "Encounter Church" in Calhoun, GA, returning to the community that had initially rejected him.

Through this tumultuous journey, he learned a profound lesson: honesty and integrity must never be sacrificed, regardless of the cost.

Standing Firm in the Face of Opposition

In a world that is constantly changing and evolving, it can be difficult to stay true to your beliefs and values, especially when those beliefs are at odds with the prevailing attitudes of society or even the religious institution to which you belong. However, history is filled with examples of men who stood firm in their faith, even when faced with fierce opposition and persecution. These men serve as inspirational examples for us today, showing us that it is possible to stand for what is right, even when it is unpopular or difficult.

One such example of a man of faith who stood firm in the face of opposition is Martin Luther. Luther, a German monk and theologian, is best known for his role in the Protestant Reformation, a movement that sought to reform the practices of the Catholic Church in the 16th century. Luther's decision to speak out against the corruption and abuses of the church was not an easy one, as he faced fierce opposition from the highest authorities in the church, including the Pope himself. However, Luther remained steadfast in his convictions, refusing to recant his beliefs even when faced with excommunication and the threat of death. Through his courage and determination, Luther sparked a revolution in the church that forever changed the course of Christianity.

Another man of faith who stood firm in the face of opposition is Dietrich Bonhoeffer. Bonhoeffer was a German Lutheran pastor and theologian who openly opposed the Nazi regime during World War II. He was a vocal critic of Hitler and his policies, particularly his persecution of the Jewish people. Bonhoeffer's resistance to the Nazi regime eventually led to his arrest and imprisonment, and he was ultimately executed in a concentration camp just days before the end of the war. Despite the risks and consequences, Bonhoeffer never wavered in his commitment to standing up for what was right, and his legacy continues to inspire people around the world today.

These men of faith serve as powerful examples for us today, reminding us that it is possible to stand firm in our convictions, even when faced with fierce opposition. They teach us that true faith requires courage, determination, and a willingness to stand up for what is right, no matter the cost. In a world that often values conformity over conviction, we must look to these men as role models, learning from their example and following in their footsteps.

In today's society, there are still many challenges facing those who seek to stand firm in their faith. Religious institutions may have their own agendas and beliefs that may not always align with the teachings of the Bible or the convictions of individual believers. In these situations, it can be difficult to know how to navigate the complexities of faith and institution, and to stand for what is right in the face of opposition.

One key lesson we can learn from men like Luther, Bonhoeffer and Davis is the importance of being grounded in the Word of God. By staying true to the teachings of Scripture and seeking guidance from the Holy Spirit, we can have confidence in our beliefs and convictions, even when they are at odds with those around us. The Bible is our ultimate authority, and it is our duty as Christians to defend its truths, even when it means standing against the religious institution itself.

Another important lesson we can learn from these men is the power of community and fellowship. Luther, Bonhoeffer and Davis were able to stand firm in their faith because they had the support of like-minded believers who stood by their side through thick and thin. In times of opposition and persecution, it is crucial to surround ourselves with fellow believers who can encourage us, pray for us, and hold us accountable in our faith journey. Together, we can stand united in our convictions, knowing that we are not alone in our struggle.

Ultimately, standing firm in our faith requires a deep and unwavering trust in God. We must believe that He is sovereign over all things, and that He will never abandon us or forsake us, even in the face of persecution or opposition. As the psalmist writes, "The Lord is my light and my salvation; whom shall I fear? The Lord is the stronghold of my life; of whom shall I be afraid?" (Psalm 27:1). With God as our fortress and our strength, we can stand firm in our faith, knowing that He is with us every step of the way.

Men of faith throughout history have shown us that it is possible to stand firm in our convictions, even when faced with fierce opposition and persecution. By following in their footsteps, we can learn to be courageous, determined, and unwavering in our commitment to what is right. As we navigate the challenges of our modern world, may we look to these men as examples of true faith and inspiration, standing firm in the face of adversity and trusting in the power of God to sustain us. Let us be men of faith, bold and unshakable, standing for what is right, even when the religious institution is against us.

Standing Firm in the Face of Compromise

As Christians, we are called to live lives of integrity and righteousness, following the example of Jesus Christ. However, there are times when we are faced with difficult choices that may require us to compromise our values in order to please others or avoid conflict. In these moments, it can be tempting to take the easy way out and compromise our integrity, but as men of faith, we are called to stand firm in our beliefs and trust in God's plan for our lives.

One of the greatest examples of standing firm in the face of compromise is found in the book of Daniel in the Bible. Daniel and his three friends, Shadrach, Meshach, and Abednego, were taken captive and brought to Babylon by King Nebuchadnezzar. Despite the temptations and pressures of living in a foreign land with a culture that was in direct conflict with their beliefs, Daniel and his friends remained faithful to God and refused to compromise their values.

One of the most well-known stories from the book of Daniel is the story of Shadrach, Meshach, and Abednego and the fiery furnace. King Nebuchadnezzar had erected a golden statue and decreed that all the people must bow down and worship it. Shadrach, Meshach, and Abednego, however, refused to bow down to the statue, as it went against their beliefs in the one true God. When they were brought before the king and given a final chance to bow down, they boldly declared, "If we are thrown into the blazing furnace, the God we serve is able to deliver us from it, and he will deliver us from Your Majesty's hand." (Daniel 3:17).

As a result of their refusal to compromise their faith, Shadrach, Meshach, and Abednego were thrown into the fiery furnace. However, to the amazement of all who witnessed it, they were not harmed by the flames. In fact, they were joined by a fourth figure in the furnace, who was described as "a son of the gods" (Daniel 3:25). The king, upon seeing this miraculous event, declared, "Praise be to the God of Shadrach, Meshach, and Abednego, who has sent his angel and rescued his servants! They trusted in him and defied the king's command and were willing to give up their lives rather than serve or worship any god except their own God." (Daniel 3:28).

The story of Shadrach, Meshach, and Abednego serves as a powerful reminder of the importance of standing firm in our faith even when we are demanded to compromise. It is easy to give in to pressure and go along with the crowd, but as men of faith, we are called to be set apart and live lives that reflect our beliefs in God. Like Daniel and his friends, we must trust in God's plan for our lives and have faith that he will deliver us from any difficult situation we may face.

Another example of standing firm in the face of compromise is found in the life of Joseph in the Old Testament. Joseph was sold into slavery by his jealous brothers and taken to Egypt, where he eventually rose to a position of power in Potiphar's household. Despite facing numerous temptations and trials, Joseph remained faithful to God and refused to compromise his integrity. When Potiphar's wife tried to seduce him, Joseph resisted her advances, declaring, "How then could I do such a wicked thing and sin against God?" (Genesis 39:9).

As a result of his refusal to compromise, Joseph was falsely accused and thrown into prison. However, even in the midst of his suffering, Joseph remained faithful to God and continued to trust in his plan for his life. Eventually, Joseph was released from prison and appointed as the second-in-command in all of Egypt, where he played a crucial role in saving his family from famine.

The story of Joseph is a powerful reminder that when we stand firm in our faith and refuse to compromise our integrity, God will honor our commitment and bless us in ways we could never imagine. It may be difficult to remain faithful in the face of compromise, but as men of faith, we are called to trust in God's plan for our lives and have faith that he will deliver us from any situation we may face.

As men of faith, we are called to stand firm in our beliefs and refuse to compromise our integrity, even in the face of pressure and temptation. The stories of Daniel, Shadrach, Meshach, Abednego, and Joseph serve as powerful reminders of the importance of trusting in God's plan for our lives and having faith that he will deliver us from any difficult situation we may face. Let us be like these men of faith and boldly declare our allegiance to God, no matter what challenges may come our way.

Like the men of faith mentioned throughout this book, Pastor Bryan Davis exhibited exemplary faith and stood in the face of compromise and held true to his integrity. We should all strive to live like this man of faith.

Chapter 12

The Action of Faith

In the Bible, we are surrounded by examples of men of faith who stepped out in obedience and trust in God. These men were not just passive believers, but they took action based on their faith in God. In this chapter, we will explore the importance of taking action in our faith and how we can follow the example of these men of faith.

The book of Hebrews is often referred to as the "Hall of Faith" because it contains a list of men and women who demonstrated great faith in God. In Hebrews 11:1, it says, "Now faith is confidence in what we hope for and assurance about what we do not see." This verse sets the foundation for understanding faith – it is not just a belief, but it is a confident assurance in God and His promises.

One of the first men of faith mentioned in Hebrews 11 is Abel. In Genesis 4, we read about Abel offering a sacrifice to God that was pleasing to Him. Abel's faith was demonstrated through his actions – he offered the best of his flock to God, showing his obedience and trust in God's provision. Because of his faith, Abel's offering was accepted by God, and he was commended as a righteous man.

Another example of faith in action is Noah. In Genesis 6, we read about how God instructed Noah to build an ark because He was going to send a flood to destroy the earth. Despite the ridicule and disbelief of those around him, Noah obeyed God and built the ark. It took years of hard work and dedication, but Noah trusted in God's promise of salvation, and his faith was rewarded when the flood came and he and his family were saved.

Abraham is perhaps one of the greatest examples of faith in action in the Bible. In Genesis 12, God called Abraham to leave his homeland and go to a land that He would show him. Abraham obeyed God without question and embarked on a journey of faith. Throughout Abraham's life, he faced many challenges and trials, but he remained steadfast in his trust in God. In Hebrews 11:17-19, it says, "By faith Abraham, when God tested him, offered Isaac as a sacrifice. He who had embraced the promises was about to sacrifice his one and only son, even though God had said to him, 'It is through Isaac that your offspring will be reckoned.' Abraham reasoned that God could even raise the dead, and so in a manner of speaking he did receive Isaac back from death." Abraham's faith was not just a passive belief – it was an active trust in God that led him to take radical steps of obedience.

The story of "avid and Goliath in 1 Samuel 17 is another powerful example of faith in action. When the Israelites were facing the giant Philistine warrior Goliath, no one in the army was willing to challenge him except for a young shepherd boy named David. Despite the odds stacked against him, David trusted in God's strength and defeated Goliath with just a sling and a stone. David's faith and courage in the face of adversity are a reminder of the power of faith in action.

In the New Testament, we see that the disciples of Jesus exemplified faith in action. In Matthew 14, we read about how Peter stepped out of the boat to walk on water towards Jesus. Despite the storm raging around him, Peter kept his eyes on Jesus and walked on water until he began to doubt and sink. Even though Peter faltered, his willingness to take a step of faith and trust in Jesus is a powerful example for us to follow.

In James 2:14-26, it says, "What good is it, my brothers and sisters, if someone claims to have faith but has no deeds? Can such faith save them? Suppose a brother or a sister is without clothes and daily food. If one of you says to them, 'Go in peace; keep warm and well fed,' but does nothing about their physical needs, what good is it? In the same way, faith by itself, if it is not accompanied by action, is dead." This passage emphasizes the importance of faith being accompanied by action. Our faith in God should lead us to do good works and make a difference in the world around us.

As men of faith, we are called to live out our beliefs through our actions. This means stepping out in obedience, trusting in God's promises, and serving others in love. We are not called to be passive spectators, but active participants in God's kingdom work.

The men of faith in the Bible serve as powerful examples for us to follow. Their stories remind us that faith is not just a belief, but it is a confident assurance in God that leads us to take action. Like Abel, Noah, Abraham, David, Peter, and the disciples, let us step out in faith and obedience, trusting in God's faithfulness and His promises. May we be men of faith who are known for our actions and our willingness to follow God wherever He may lead us.

Our actions show our fruits as men of faith. As Christians, we are called to live a life that reflects the love and teachings of Jesus Christ. Our actions are a manifestation of our faith and beliefs, and they can have a powerful impact on those around us.

In the book of Matthew, Jesus tells us that a tree is known by its fruit. In the same way, our actions can reveal the true nature of our faith. Are we living in accordance with the principles of love, compassion, and forgiveness that Jesus taught? Or are we displaying selfishness, anger, and judgment towards others?

As men of faith, it is essential that our actions align with our beliefs. We cannot claim to be followers of Christ and yet live a life that is contrary to his teachings. Our words and actions must be in harmony with the values of the gospel, showing love and kindness to all those we encounter.

One of the clearest indicators of our faith is how we treat others. Are we quick to judge and condemn, or do we offer grace and forgiveness? Are we actively seeking to help those in need, or are we turning a blind eye to the suffering around us? Our actions towards others reveal the true depth of our faith and our commitment to following the example of Jesus.

In the book of James, we are reminded that faith without works is dead. It is not enough to simply believe in God; we must also live out our faith through our actions. This means actively serving others, showing kindness and compassion, and striving to make a positive impact in the world around us.

Our actions as men of faith should also reflect the fruit of the spirit, as outlined in Galatians 5:22-23. These fruits include love, joy, peace, patience, kindness, goodness, faithfulness, gentleness, and self-control. When we exhibit these qualities in our interactions with others, we are demonstrating the presence of the Holy Spirit within us.

Furthermore, our actions should also reflect the character of Christ. Jesus was known for his humility, compassion, and selflessness. As men of faith, we should strive to emulate these qualities in our own lives, putting the needs of others before our own and treating all people with dignity and respect.

Our actions truly do show our fruits as men of faith. It is not enough to simply profess belief in Christ; we must also live out our faith through our words and deeds. By embodying the values of the gospel, serving others with love and compassion, and reflecting the character of

Christ in all that we do, we can truly be shining examples of what it means to be men of faith. May our actions speak louder than our words and bear witness to the transformative power of God's love in our lives.

All throughout the Bible, we read about many men who exhibited great faith in God. These men relied on God's promises, trusted in His timing, and lived their lives in obedience to His will. Their stories serve as a powerful example for us today, encouraging us to grow in our own faith and trust in the Lord.

One of the key qualities of men of faith is their unwavering trust in God. They believe in His power and sovereignty, knowing that He is in control of all things. In the book of Hebrews, we read about Abraham, who was called to leave his homeland and travel to a land that God would show him. Despite not knowing where he was going, Abraham trusted in God's guiding hand and followed Him faithfully. His faith was credited to him as righteousness, and he became known as the father of faith.

Like Abraham, men of faith are willing to step out in obedience to God, even when it seems uncertain or difficult. They are not afraid to take risks or make sacrifices for the sake of following God's will. This level of faith requires courage and a willingness to trust in God's goodness, no matter what the circumstances may be.

Another quality of men of faith is their perseverance in the face of challenges and trials. In the book of James, we read about Job, a man who endured immense suffering and loss, yet remained faithful to God. Despite his friends' accusations and his own doubts, Job held fast to his faith, trusting that God's ultimate plan was beyond his understanding.

Men of faith understand that their faith will be tested and refined in the fires of adversity. They know that hardship and trials are an opportunity for growth and maturity in their walk with the Lord. Instead of becoming bitter and resentful, they choose to lean on God's grace and seek His strength to help them endure.

Moreover, men of faith demonstrate humility and dependence on God. They recognize that they are nothing without Him and that every good thing comes from His hand. Like David, who was described as a man after God's own heart, they seek to cultivate a deep relationship with Him through prayer, worship, and obedience.

Men of faith also exhibit a spirit of generosity and compassion. They understand the importance of caring for others and showing love to those in need. In the New Testament, we read about Paul, who traveled far and wide to share the message of salvation with those who had not yet heard it. His passion for spreading the gospel was fueled by his love for God and his desire to see others come to faith.

Men of faith are characterized by their unwavering trust in God, perseverance in the face of challenges, humility and dependence on Him, and a spirit of generosity and compassion. Their lives serve as a powerful testimony to the faithfulness and goodness of God, inspiring us to grow in our own faith and trust in Him. May we strive to emulate their example and live lives that bring glory and honor to the Lord.

The Generosity of Faith

In the world we live in today, generosity is often seen as a rare and precious virtue. We are bombarded with messages of materialism and selfishness, and the idea of giving selflessly can sometimes seem like a foreign concept. However, for those who walk in faith, generosity is not just a nice gesture – it is a way of life.

In the Bible, we are told that "it is more blessed to give than to receive" (Acts 20:35). This simple statement encapsulates the heart of generosity – it is not about what we can get, but rather about what we can give. As men of faith, we are called to embody this principle in our daily lives, and to show the world the true meaning of generosity.

One of the greatest examples of generosity in the Bible is the story of the widow's mite. In Mark 12:41-44, Jesus watches as wealthy people put large sums of money into the temple treasury, but it is the widow who gives two small coins who catches his eye. Jesus praises her, saying that she has given more than all the others because she gave out of her poverty, while the others gave out of their wealth. This story teaches us that true generosity is not measured by the size of the gift, but by the heart that gives it.

As men of faith, we are called to give generously, not just of our wealth, but of our time, talents, and resources. We are called to be blessings to those around us, to serve others selflessly, and to give cheerfully and willingly. In 2 Corinthians 9:6-8, we are reminded that "whoever sows sparingly will also reap sparingly, and whoever sows generously will also reap generously." When we give generously, we not only bless others, but we also open ourselves up to be blessed in return.

Generosity is not just about giving money or material possessions – it is about giving of ourselves. It is about showing love and kindness to those in need, and being a beacon of hope in a world that is often dark and filled with despair. When we give generously, we reflect the heart of God, who gave us his Son, Jesus Christ, as the ultimate gift of love and grace.

As men of faith, we are called to be stewards of the blessings that God has given us, and to use those blessings to bless others. We are called to be generous not just when it is convenient or easy, but at all times and in all circumstances. We are called to be like the Good Samaritan, who went out of his way to help a stranger in need, showing mercy and compassion without expecting anything in return.

In Matthew 25:31-46, Jesus tells the parable of the sheep and the goats, in which he separates the righteous from the unrighteous based on how they treated the least of his brothers and sisters. The righteous are commended for their acts of kindness and generosity, while the unrighteous are condemned for their lack of compassion. This parable reminds us that our generosity towards others is a reflection of our faith in God, and that our actions have eternal consequences.

As men of faith, we are called to be generous in all aspects of our lives – in our relationships, in our work, and in our community. We are called to be generous with our forgiveness, our patience, and our grace. We are called to be generous with our words, our prayers, and our encouragement. We are called to be generous with our time, our talents, and our resources. In short, we are called to be generous in all things, just as our Heavenly Father is generous to us.

Generosity is not just a virtue – it is a way of life for men of faith. We are called to be generous in all things, reflecting the love and grace of our Heavenly Father to those around us. As we give generously, we not only bless others, but we also bless ourselves, for "whoever sows generously will also reap generously." Let us strive to be men of faith who are known for our generosity, and who leave a legacy of love and kindness for generations to come.

Chapter 13

Freedom in Faith

It can be difficult to find solace and peace. However, for men of faith, there is a deep sense of freedom that comes from placing their trust in God. In this chapter, we will explore the concept of freedom in faith and how it empowers men to live boldly and fearlessly in the midst of life's challenges.

Many men of faith have experienced the transformative power of surrendering their lives to God. This act of relinquishing control can be daunting, as it requires a great deal of trust and faith. However, once men are able to let go of their own desires and plans, they find a newfound sense of freedom in knowing that they are not alone in their journey.

One of the key aspects of freedom in faith is the ability to trust in God's plan for one's life. Men of faith understand that God has a unique purpose and calling for each individual, and they are able to surrender to this divine plan with confidence. This trust allows them to let go of their own expectations and fears, knowing that God's will is ultimately what is best for them.

In addition to trust, men of faith also experience freedom from fear. The world can be a scary and unpredictable place, but those who have faith in God are able to face their fears with courage and strength. This sense of fearlessness comes from knowing that God is always with them, guiding and protecting them in all circumstances.

Furthermore, freedom in faith allows men to break free from the constraints of the world and live according to God's values and principles. In a society that often promotes selfishness, materialism, and instant gratification, men of faith are able to rise above these temptations and live with integrity, honesty, and compassion. This freedom from societal pressures allows them to live with purpose and meaning, knowing that they are following God's will for their lives.

Men of faith also experience freedom in forgiveness. It can be difficult to let go of past hurts and resentments, but through faith, men are able to extend forgiveness to others and themselves. This act of forgiveness brings about healing and restoration, allowing men to move forward with a renewed sense of peace and freedom.

Freedom in faith enables men to live with a sense of hope and optimism. In a world filled with despair and negativity, men of faith are able to look towards the future with confidence, knowing that God has a plan for their lives and that all things will work together for good. This hope allows them to face each day with joy and gratitude, despite the challenges that may come their way.

Freedom in faith is a powerful concept that empowers men to live boldly and fearlessly in a world that is often filled with uncertainty and chaos. Through trust, fearlessness, integrity, forgiveness, and hope, men of faith are able to experience a deep sense of freedom that comes from knowing that they are loved and guided by God. As men continue to walk in faith, they will find that this freedom allows them to live with purpose, meaning, and fulfillment, knowing that they are following God's will for their lives.

In a world that seems to be constantly putting us in chains of fear, doubt, and worry, walking in freedom with faith is crucial for every Christian man. As men of faith, we are called to live our lives boldly and confidently, knowing that our God is with us every step of the way. So what it means to walk in freedom with faith and how can we live out this calling in our daily lives?

One of the key aspects of walking in freedom with faith is understanding the power of belief. As men of faith, we must believe in the promises of God and trust in His plan for our lives. This belief is not just a passive acceptance of facts, but an active and intentional choice to trust in God's goodness and faithfulness. When we truly believe in God's promises, we can walk in freedom, knowing that He will always be there to guide and protect us.

Another important aspect of walking in freedom with faith is letting go of our fears and insecurities. As men, we are often taught to be strong and independent, but this mindset can sometimes lead to pride and self-reliance. Instead, we must learn to surrender our fears and insecurities to God, trusting in His strength and wisdom to carry us through difficult times.

Walking in freedom with faith also requires us to cultivate a spirit of gratitude and praise. When we focus on the blessings in our lives and give thanks to God for His goodness, we are reminded of His faithfulness and provision. This spirit of gratitude helps us to have a more positive outlook on life and allows us to walk in freedom, knowing that God is in control.

As men of faith, we are called to be bold and courageous in our walk with God. This means stepping out in faith, even when the path ahead seems uncertain or daunting. When we trust in God's promises and take bold steps of faith, we can experience true freedom in Christ, knowing that He will never leave us or forsake us.

Walking in freedom with faith also requires us to stay connected to God through prayer and meditation on His Word. By staying rooted in scripture and spending time in prayer, we can draw closer to God and receive the guidance and strength we need to walk in freedom. Prayer and meditation help us to cultivate a deeper relationship with God and align our hearts with His will for our lives.

Walking in freedom with faith is a journey that requires courage, trust, and perseverance. As men of faith, we are called to live boldly and confidently, knowing that our God is with us every step of the way. By believing in God's promises, letting go of our fears and insecurities, cultivating a spirit of gratitude and praise, being bold and courageous, and staying connected to God through prayer and meditation, we can walk in freedom with faith and experience the abundant life that Christ has promised us. Let us rise up as men of faith and live out our calling with strength and conviction, knowing that God is always by our side.

In our journey as men of faith, we are called to live in the freedom that faith brings. This freedom is not just a concept or a theory, but a reality that we can experience in our daily lives. It is the freedom to live fully and abundantly, to be who we were created to be, and to embrace all that God has for us.

The Bible tells us in Galatians 5:1, "It is for freedom that Christ has set us free. Stand firm, then, and do not let yourselves be burdened again by a yoke of slavery." This verse reminds us that as believers in Christ, we have been set free from the bondage of sin and death. We no longer have to carry the weight of our past mistakes, failures, or insecurities. Instead, we can walk in the freedom that comes from knowing Christ and trusting in His promises.

Walking in faith means trusting in God's plan for our lives and believing that He has good things in store for us. It means surrendering our fears, doubts, and worries to Him, and allowing Him to guide us on the path He has laid out for us. When we walk in faith, we can experience the abundance of life that God intends for us.

In John 10:10, Jesus says, "The thief comes only to steal and kill and destroy; I have come that they may have life, and have it to the full." This verse reminds us that the enemy wants to steal our joy, kill our dreams, and destroy our faith. But Jesus came to give us abundant life – a life filled with purpose, peace, and prosperity. When we walk in faith, we can claim this abundant life for ourselves.

One of the key aspects of walking in faith is trusting in God's provision. The Bible tells us in Matthew 6:33, "But seek first his kingdom and his righteousness, and all these things will be given to you as well." This verse reminds us that when we put our trust in God and seek His will above all else, He will provide for all of our needs. We don't have to worry about where our next meal will come from, or how we will pay our bills, because God is faithful to provide for us.

Walking in faith also means stepping out of our comfort zones and taking risks for the sake of the Gospel. It means being willing to go where God leads us, even if it means facing opposition, persecution, or hardship. The

Bible tells us in Hebrews 11:6, "And without faith it is impossible to please God, because anyone who comes to him must believe that he exists and that he rewards those who earnestly seek him." This verse reminds us that faith requires action – it requires us to step out in obedience and trust that God will reward our efforts.

As men of faith, we are called to be bold and courageous in our walk with God. We are called to be leaders in our families, communities, and churches, and to set an example of faithfulness and obedience to those around us. We are called to be men of integrity, humility, and compassion – reflecting the character of Christ in all that we do.

Walking in the freedom of faith brings us the abundance of life that God intends for us. It allows us to experience the fullness of His blessings and promises, and to live with purpose and passion. As men of faith, let us embrace this freedom with courage and conviction, trusting in God's provision and stepping out in obedience to His call. Let us be men who walk in faith, knowing that our God is faithful to fulfill His promises and lead us into a life of abundance and joy.

In today's world, where integrity seems to be a rare quality, it is important for men of faith to not only uphold their beliefs but also walk in the freedom that faith provides. As Christians, we are called to live our lives with integrity, honesty, and righteousness in all that we do. I want to emphasize the importance of walking in the freedom of faith in order to produce integrity in our lives.

What is Integrity?

Integrity is defined as the quality of being honest and having strong moral principles. It is the adherence to a code of moral values, doing what is right even when no one is looking. Integrity is essential in all aspects of our lives, including our relationships, work, and personal conduct.

As men of faith, we are called to be examples of integrity in a world that often lacks it. Our faith in God should guide us in our decisions and actions, leading us to live with honesty and righteousness. When we walk in the freedom of faith, we are able to truly embody integrity in all that we do.

The Freedom of Faith

Faith is a powerful force that can move mountains and change lives. It is the belief in God's promises and the trust that He will guide us in all things. When we have faith, we are set free from fear, doubt, and worry, allowing us to live with confidence and courage.

Walking in the freedom of faith means trusting in God's plan for our lives and surrendering our will to His. It allows us to let go of our own desires and ambitions, and instead focus on following God's will for us. In this freedom, we are able to live with purpose and meaning, knowing that God is in control of all things.

Integrity Through Faith

When we walk in the freedom of faith, we are able to produce integrity in our lives in several ways. Firstly, faith instills in us a sense of responsibility and accountability. We understand that our actions have consequences, and we strive to do what is right in all situations.

Secondly, faith promotes honesty and transparency. When we trust in God, we are able to be open and truthful in our dealings with others. We do not need to hide our mistakes or shortcomings, but instead can confess them and seek forgiveness and reconciliation.

Finally, faith produces integrity through our relationships with others. When we walk in the freedom of faith, we are able to treat others with respect, kindness, and love. We do not manipulate or deceive others for our own gain, but instead seek to build them up and encourage them in their faith.

Living With Integrity

As men of faith, we are called to live with integrity in all aspects of our lives. This means being honest and truthful in our words and actions, treating others with respect and kindness, and following God's will for us with obedience and humility. It is only through walking in the freedom of faith that we can truly produce integrity in our lives.

Walking in the freedom of faith produces integrity in our lives. As men of faith, we are called to live with honesty, righteousness, and moral principles in all that we do. By trusting in God's plan for us and surrendering our will to His, we are able to walk in the freedom that faith provides and live with integrity in all aspects of our lives. Let us strive to be men of faith who uphold our beliefs and walk with integrity in a world that desperately needs it.

Chapter 14

The Conviction of Faith

Faith is an essential aspect of the Christian life. It is the foundation upon which we build our relationship with God and navigate through the challenges and uncertainties of life. In the Bible, we are given numerous examples of men who exhibited great faith in God and trusted Him in the midst of adversity. These men of faith serve as role models for us today, showing us what it means to have a deep conviction of faith.

One such man of faith is Abraham. In the book of Genesis, we read about how God called Abraham to leave his homeland and go to a place that He would show him. Despite the uncertainty and risks involved, Abraham obeyed God's command and embarked on a journey of faith. Throughout his life, Abraham faced many trials and struggles, but he never wavered in his faith in God. His conviction of faith was so strong that he was willing to sacrifice his own son, Isaac, in obedience to God's command. In the end, God provided a ram as a substitute for Isaac, demonstrating His faithfulness and provision to those who trust Him.

Another man of faith is Job. In the book of Job, we read about how Job lost everything he had – his wealth, his health, and even his family. Despite his immense suffering, Job maintained his faith in God and refused to curse Him. Job's friends tried to convince him that his suffering was a result of his sin, but Job remained steadfast in his belief that God was sovereign and wise. In the end, God restored Job's fortunes and blessed him even more than before. Job's story serves as a powerful reminder that faith in God is not dependent on our circumstances, but on our trust in His goodness and sovereignty.

David is another man of faith who demonstrated great conviction in his relationship with God. As a young shepherd boy, David faced the giant Goliath with nothing but a sling and a stone. Despite the overwhelming odds against him, David trusted in God to deliver him and defeat his enemy. Throughout his life, David faced many trials and challenges, but he never lost his faith in God. In times of trouble, David turned to God in prayer and sought His guidance and strength. David's psalms are a testament to his deep relationship with God and his unwavering trust in His faithfulness.

These men of faith teach us valuable lessons about what it means to have a conviction of faith. They show us that faith is not just a belief in God's existence, but a deep trust in His character and promises. Faith is not just a feeling, but a conscious choice to trust God in all circumstances. Faith is not just for the good times, but for the hard times as well. Like Abraham, Job, and David, we are called to have a steadfast faith that endures through trials and tribulations.

In our modern world, where skepticism and doubt abound, we are called to be men of faith who stand firm in our convictions. We are called to be like Abraham, who trusted God's promise of a son even when it seemed impossible. We are called to be like Job, who maintained his faith in God's goodness even in the midst of suffering. We are called to be like David, who sought God's strength and guidance in times of trouble. As men of faith, we are called to be a light in a dark world, showing others the power of trust and obedience in God.

The conviction of faith is a hallmark of the Christian life. Men of faith like Abraham, Job, and David exemplify what it means to trust in God wholeheartedly and to walk in obedience to His commands. Their stories inspire us to have a deep conviction of faith that endures through trials and tribulations. As we strive to be men of faith in our own lives, may we learn from the examples of these great men and trust in God's faithfulness and goodness. May we walk in the footsteps of faith, knowing that He who calls us is faithful and will fulfill His promises in His perfect timing.

In today's culture, it can be challenging to stand firm in our beliefs and convictions as Christians. The pressures and temptations of society can often pull us away from the path that God has set before us. However, as men of faith, it is crucial that we not only believe in our convictions but also live them out in our daily lives.

Living out our convictions as men of faith requires courage, discipline, and a strong commitment to following God's will. It means being willing to say no to the things that go against our beliefs and values, even when it is difficult or unpopular. It means standing up for what is right, even when we are faced with opposition or criticism. It means being an example of Christ's love and grace in every aspect of our lives.

One of the key components of living out our convictions as men of faith is being rooted in the Word of God. The Bible is our guidebook for living a life that is pleasing to God, and it is essential that we spend time studying and meditating on its teachings. By immersing ourselves in

Scripture, we can gain a deeper understanding of God's will for our lives and be better equipped to follow it.

Another important aspect of living out our convictions as men of faith is being in community with other like-minded believers. Surrounding ourselves with fellow Christians who can encourage, support, and hold us accountable in our walk with God is crucial for staying strong in our convictions. The Bible tells us in Hebrews 10:24-25, "And let us consider how we may spur one another on toward love and good deeds, not giving up meeting together, as some are in the habit of doing, but encouraging one another—and all the more as you see the Day approaching."

Living out our convictions as men of faith also requires us to be intentional about our actions and choices. It means being mindful of the way we conduct ourselves in our relationships, at work, and in our communities. It means being a man of integrity, honesty, and compassion, reflecting the character of Christ in all that we do.

In his letter to the Colossians, the apostle Paul exhorts believers to "put on the new self, which is being renewed in knowledge in the image of its Creator" (Colossians 3:10). This new self is marked by qualities such as kindness, compassion, humility, gentleness, and patience. As men of faith, it is our calling to embody these virtues in our interactions with others, showing the love of Christ to a world in desperate need of it.

Living out our convictions as men of faith also means being willing to stand up for what is right, even when it may cost us something. In the book of Daniel, we read about the prophet's unwavering commitment to God's laws, even in the face of intense pressure to conform to the pagan practices of the Babylonian empire. Daniel's example serves as a powerful reminder that we must be willing to take a stand for our beliefs, regardless of the consequences.

As men of faith, we are called to be bold and courageous in our witness for Christ, sharing the hope and truth of the Gospel with a world that is lost and in need of salvation. This may involve stepping out of our comfort zones, speaking up in the face of injustice, or taking a stand against the prevailing cultural norms. It may require us to make sacrifices and endure hardship for the sake of the Kingdom of God. But in the end, the reward of faithfulness to our convictions is eternal, as Paul reminds us in 2 Timothy 4:7-8, "I have fought the good fight, I have finished the race, I have kept the faith. Now there is in store for me the crown of righteousness, which the Lord, the righteous Judge, will award to me on that day—and not only to me, but also to all who have longed for his appearing."

Living out our convictions as men of faith is not always easy, but it is essential for fulfilling our calling as followers of Christ. It requires us to be rooted in God's Word, in community with other believers, and intentional in our actions and choices. It means being willing to stand up for what is right, even in the face of adversity. And ultimately, it means being bold and courageous in our witness for Christ, proclaiming the truth of the Gospel to a world in need of redemption. May we, as men of faith, strive to live out our convictions with integrity, obedience, and a steadfast commitment to following God's will in all that we do.

Men of faith are often looked upon as pillars of strength and steadfastness in the Christian community. They are seen as examples of boldness, courage, and unwavering faith in the face of adversity. But what happens when even these men of faith ignore their convictions and stray from the path that God has set before them?

In the Bible, we see numerous examples of men who, despite their strong faith, faltered and made mistakes when they ignored their convictions. One such example is King David, a man after God's own heart who committed adultery with Bathsheba and orchestrated the death of her husband Uriah. Despite his deep faith and close relationship with God, David allowed his desires to overtake him and ignored the convictions that he knew to be true.

Another example is Peter, one of Jesus' closest disciples. Peter boldly proclaimed his loyalty to Jesus, even going as far as to say that he would never deny him. But when faced with the threat of persecution, Peter denied knowing Jesus three times. He ignored his convictions and gave in to fear, failing to stand firm in his faith.

These examples serve as a reminder that even the strongest men of faith are not immune to temptation and sin. When we ignore our convictions, we open ourselves up to the enemy's attacks and risk straying from the path that God has set before us.

Ignoring our convictions can lead to a downward spiral of sin and disobedience. When we choose to ignore the still, small voice of the Holy Spirit prompting us to do what is right, we are placing ourselves in a dangerous position. The enemy will use our weaknesses and vulnerabilities to lead us astray and separate us from God.

So how can we, as men of faith, avoid ignoring our convictions and stay true to the path that God has set before us?

First and foremost, we must cultivate a deep and intimate relationship with God through prayer, study of His Word, and fellowship with other believers. By staying connected to God, we can be constantly reminded of His truth and guidance in our lives.

Secondly, we must be vigilant and mindful of the temptations and distractions that surround us. The enemy is always seeking to deceive and lead us away from God, so we must be on guard and stand firm in our faith.

Thirdly, we must surround ourselves with accountability partners who will hold us to a high standard and help us stay on track. By having a support system of fellow believers who can encourage, challenge, and correct us when we stray from our convictions, we can avoid falling into the traps of sin and disobedience.

Finally, we must be willing to humble ourselves and seek forgiveness when we do falter and ignore our convictions. God is always ready to forgive and restore us when we repent and turn back to Him. By acknowledging our mistakes and seeking reconciliation with God and others, we can experience the healing and restoration that comes from true repentance.

Men of faith are not immune to temptation and sin. When we ignore our convictions, we open ourselves up to the enemy's attacks and risk straying from the path that God has set before us. By cultivating a deep relationship with God, being vigilant of temptations, surrounding ourselves with accountability partners, and humbling ourselves in repentance, we can avoid ignoring our convictions and stay true to the faith that God has called us to. Let us be men of faith who stand firm in our convictions and boldly proclaim the truth of God's love and grace to the world.

Chapter 15

The Consequences of Living Without Faith

In the vast tapestry of history, there have been countless men and women who have stood as beacons of faith. From Noah and Abraham to David and Paul, these men of faith have inspired generations with their unwavering trust in the Almighty.

But what about those who choose to live without faith? What are the consequences of rejecting the divine and seeking solace in the material world alone? In this chapter, we will explore the dangers and pitfalls of living a faithless existence, and the profound impact it can have on individuals and society as a whole.

The Absence of Hope

One of the most devastating consequences of living without faith is the absence of hope. When one rejects God's will in their life and dismisses the notion of divine intervention, they are left to navigate the trials and tribulations of life alone.

Without faith, there is no belief in a greater purpose or meaning to our existence. This can lead to feelings of despair and hopelessness, as individuals struggle to find a sense of direction and purpose in a world that can often seem cruel and indifferent.

In times of hardship and adversity, it is faith that provides a beacon of hope, a light in the darkness that guides us through the storm. Without this faith, individuals may find themselves adrift, lost in a sea of uncertainty and doubt.

The Dangers of Reliance on Self

Living without faith can also lead to an over-reliance on oneself and one's own abilities. When one rejects God, they may come to believe that they are the masters of their own destiny, with no need for outside guidance or support.

This can lead to a dangerous sense of arrogance and pride, as individuals believe that they alone are responsible for their successes and failures. Without the humility that comes from recognizing the limitations of one's own abilities, individuals may find themselves blindsided by their own shortcomings and weaknesses.

In contrast, men of faith understand that their strength comes from the Almighty, and that it is through His grace and guidance that they are able to overcome life's challenges. By placing their trust in God, they are able to tap into a source of infinite wisdom and strength that far surpasses their own.

The Erosion of Moral Values

Living without faith can also lead to the erosion of moral values and ethical principles. When one rejects God and dismisses the notion of divine law, they are left to define right and wrong for themselves.

In a world where moral relativism reigns supreme, individuals may find it difficult to discern between right and wrong, good and evil. Without a firm foundation in faith, they may be swayed by the ever-changing tides of popular opinion, unable to distinguish truth from falsehood.

Men of faith, on the other hand, understand that there are objective truths that transcend human opinion. They recognize that there is a divine standard of morality that serves as a guidepost for their actions and decisions. By adhering to these timeless principles, they are able to navigate the moral complexities of life with wisdom and integrity.

The Social Impact of Faithlessness

The consequences of living without faith are not limited to individuals alone. The erosion of faith can have a profound impact on society as a whole, leading to a breakdown of moral values, social cohesion, and communal solidarity.

In a world where faith is marginalized and God is pushed to the sidelines, individuals may find it difficult to connect with one another on a deeper level. Without a shared belief in God, there is little to bind us together as a community, and we may find ourselves adrift in a sea of individualism and isolation.

Men of faith, on the other hand, understand the importance of community and fellowship. They recognize that we are all children of a loving and merciful God, bound together by a common faith and a shared commitment to serving others.

By embodying the virtues of faith, humility, and love, men of faith are able to build strong and resilient communities that are able to withstand the storms of life. Through their example, they inspire others to seek out the transcendent truths that can only be found in faith.

The consequences of living without faith are vast and far-reaching. From the erosion of hope and moral values to the breakdown of social cohesion, the absence of faith can have a devastating impact on individuals and society as a whole.

Men of faith serve as a shining example of the transformative power of belief in God. Through their unwavering trust in the Almighty, they are able to navigate life's challenges with grace and wisdom, inspiring others to seek out the transcendent truths that can only be found in faith.

As we reflect on the consequences of living without faith, may we be inspired to embrace the virtues of faith, humility, and love, and to build communities that are grounded in the timeless principles of divine law. In doing so, we can create a world that is guided by faith, hope, and love, and that is able to withstand the trials and tribulations of life with strength and grace.

In today's society, faith seems to be under attack like never before. With the rise of skepticism, materialism, and individualism, faith in God is becoming increasingly rare. I want to explore the erosion of faith in our culture and the importance of men of faith in combating this trend.

It is no secret that our society is becoming more secular with each passing day. The idea of faith in God is often ridiculed and dismissed as irrational or outdated. This skepticism is fueled by the advancements in science and technology, which have provided alternative explanations for phenomena that were once attributed to divine intervention.

Materialism also plays a significant role in the erosion of faith. The pursuit of wealth and material possessions has become the primary focus for many individuals, leaving little room for spiritual growth or belief in something beyond the material world. In a culture that values material success above all else, faith can easily be pushed to the margins.

Individualism further contributes to the erosion of faith in our culture. The emphasis on personal autonomy and self-reliance can lead individuals to believe that they have all the answers within themselves, without the need for God. This mindset can be isolating and can prevent individuals from seeking out a community of faith for support and guidance.

In the face of these challenges, men of faith are needed now more than ever. Men who have a strong belief in God and who live out their faith in their daily lives serve as beacons of hope in a world that is increasingly cynical and disenchanted. These men can inspire others to seek out a deeper connection with something greater than themselves and can provide a sense of community and support for those struggling with their own faith.

Men of faith can also serve as a counterbalance to the materialistic and individualistic tendencies of our culture. By living lives of service, generosity, and compassion, these men can demonstrate the true value of faith in God. They can show that there is more to life than the pursuit of material possessions and that true fulfillment comes from a connection to something greater than ourselves.

The erosion of faith in our culture presents a significant challenge for men of faith. However, by living out their beliefs in a genuine and authentic way, these men can serve as a powerful force for good in a world that is increasingly skeptical and disillusioned. By inspiring others to seek out a deeper connection with God and by living lives of service and compassion, men of faith can help to combat the erosion of faith in our culture and provide a beacon of hope for those in need.

Men of faith are often seen as pillars of strength and steadfastness in the Christian community. They are admired for their unwavering trust in God and their ability to overcome trials and tribulations through their faith. However, not all men who identify as Christians possess this level of faith. But what about being a faithless Christian and how can we overcome this lack of faith.

Being a faithless Christian is not uncommon. Many men struggle with doubts and uncertainties in their faith, often feeling inadequate or unworthy of God's love and grace. These feelings can be exacerbated by external challenges and hardships, leading to a crisis of faith. In times of crisis, it is easy to lose sight of God's presence and promises, causing one to question the very foundation of their belief.

One of the main reasons for a lack of faith in Christians is a lack of intimacy with God. Men who do not prioritize their relationship with God often find it difficult to trust in Him and His plan for their lives. Without a strong connection to God, doubts and fears can easily take root and hinder one's faith. In order to combat this, it is important for men to cultivate a deep and personal relationship with God through prayer, reading the Bible, and participating in fellowship with other believers.

Another contributing factor to faithlessness in Christians is the influence of the world. In today's society, it can be challenging to live out one's faith in a culture that is increasingly secular and hostile towards Christianity. Men may face ridicule, rejection, or persecution for their beliefs, causing them to shrink back and hide their faith. However, God calls us to be bold and unashamed in our faith, trusting in Him to provide strength and courage in the face of opposition.

Fear is another common obstacle to faith in Christians. Many men struggle with fear of the unknown, fear of failure, or fear of rejection, which can paralyze their faith and prevent them from fully surrendering to God. However, God reminds us that He has not given us a spirit of fear, but of power, love, and a sound mind. By relying on God's strength and promises, we can overcome our fears and step out in faith, knowing that He is with us every step of the way.

In order to combat faithlessness, men must also be vigilant in guarding their hearts and minds against doubt and unbelief. The enemy will often try to plant seeds of doubt in our minds, causing us to question God's goodness and faithfulness. However, we must take every thought captive and align it with the truth of God's Word, which promises us that He will never leave us nor forsake us.

Men of faith must remember that faith is a journey, not a destination. It is normal to experience periods of doubt and struggle in our faith, but it is important to persevere and keep pressing on towards the goal of knowing Christ more intimately. By seeking God's presence daily, surrendering our fears and doubts to Him, and surrounding ourselves with fellow believers who can encourage and support us, we can overcome faithlessness and walk boldly in the faith that God has called us to.

Being a faithless Christian is a struggle that many men face, but it is not a permanent state. By cultivating a deep relationship with God, resisting the influence of the world, overcoming fear, guarding our hearts and minds, and persevering in our faith journey, we can overcome faithlessness and become men of faith who trust wholeheartedly in God's promises and plan for our lives. God is faithful, and He will give us the strength and grace we need to walk in faith and obedience, regardless of our circumstances.

Chapter 16

Choosing Where to Place Your Trust

As men of faith, it is crucial for us to understand the power of our beliefs and where we direct them. Our faith has the ability to shape our thoughts, actions, and ultimately our destiny. Let us explore the importance of making intentional choices about where we place our trust and how it can impact our lives in profound ways.

The Bible teaches us in Hebrews 11:1 that "faith is the assurance of things hoped for, the conviction of things not seen." This verse reminds us that faith requires us to believe in something beyond what our physical eyes can perceive. It calls us to have trust and confidence in God's promises, even when we cannot see the outcome. This kind of faith is a powerful force that can move mountains and bring about miraculous transformations in our lives.

As men of faith, we must be discerning about where we place our trust. The world offers us countless distractions and temptations, seeking to pull us away from the path of righteousness and truth. We must guard our hearts and minds against the lies and deceptions that surround us, and instead fix our eyes on Jesus, the author and perfecter of our faith.

One of the key principles of faith is that what we focus on will manifest in our lives. If we choose to place our trust in God and His Word, we will bear the fruits of righteousness, peace, and joy. On the other hand, if we put our faith in worldly pursuits, material possessions, or our own abilities, we will reap a harvest of dissatisfaction, anxiety, and emptiness.

Jesus spoke about this concept in Matthew 6:33 when He said, "Seek first the Kingdom of God and His righteousness, and all these things will be added unto you." This verse reminds us that when we prioritize our relationship with God and trust in His provision, He will bless us abundantly. Our faith in God's promises will open doors of opportunity, protection, and favor that we could never achieve on our own.

In contrast, when we put our trust in the things of this world, we set ourselves up for disappointment and failure. The pursuit of wealth, success, and pleasure may offer temporary satisfaction, but it will ultimately leave us feeling empty and unfulfilled. True fulfillment can only be found in a deep and abiding relationship with our Creator, who knows us intimately and loves us unconditionally.

As men of faith, we must continually examine our hearts and minds to ensure that we are placing our trust in the right things. Are we seeking approval and validation from others, or are we secure in our identity as children of God? Are we chasing after worldly pleasures, or are we content with the peace and joy that comes from a life surrendered to Christ? Are we relying on our own strength and wisdom, or are we putting our faith in the power of the Holy Spirit to guide and empower us?

These are questions that we must ask ourselves daily, as we navigate the challenges and opportunities of life. When we make the conscious choice to place our trust in God and His promises, we will experience a transformation in our attitudes, habits, and relationships. Our faith will act as a compass, leading us towards the abundant life that Jesus promised to those who follow Him wholeheartedly.

As men of faith, we have a responsibility to choose wisely where we place our trust. Our faith has the power to shape our reality and determine our destiny. Let us fix our eyes on Jesus, the author and perfecter of our faith, and trust in His unchanging love and provision. May we be known as men of faith who bear the fruits of righteousness, peace, and joy, as we walk in obedience to God's Word and His will for our lives.

It is more important than ever to have faith in something greater than ourselves. Faith has the power to sustain us through the darkest of times, to give us hope when all seems lost, and to guide us on a path of purpose and fulfillment.

As men of faith, we are called to live our lives with intentionality – to fully embrace and embody the beliefs and values that we hold dear. It is not enough to simply believe in God and go through the motions of our faith; we must actively strive to deepen our relationship with Him, to grow in our understanding of His word, and to live out our faith in every aspect of our lives.

Intentional faith is about more than just attending church on Sundays or saying a quick prayer before bed. It is about making a conscious decision to prioritize our relationship with God, to seek His guidance and wisdom in all that we do, and to trust in His plan for our lives.

One of the key aspects of intentional faith is surrender. As men of faith, we must learn to let go of our own desires and agendas and submit ourselves fully to God's will. This can be a challenging process, as it often requires us to relinquish control and trust in God's timing and plan. But when we surrender our lives to Him, we open ourselves up to a world of possibilities and blessings that we could never have imagined.

Intentional faith also involves a commitment to spiritual growth and maturity. This means actively seeking out opportunities for learning and growth, whether it be through studying the Bible, participating in small group discussions, or attending church services and events. It also means surrounding ourselves with other like-minded individuals who can support and encourage us on our journey of faith.

As men of faith, we are called to be beacons of light and hope in a dark and broken world. We must be willing to stand firm in our beliefs, even in the face of adversity and opposition. We must be bold in sharing our faith with others, not out of a sense of obligation or duty, but out of a genuine desire to see God's love and truth transform lives.

Intentional faith is not always easy, and there will undoubtedly be times when we struggle to hold onto our beliefs in the midst of trials and tribulations. But it is during these moments of struggle that our faith is tested and refined, and our relationship with God grows stronger.

In the book of Hebrews, we are reminded of the power of faith: "Now faith is confidence in what we hope for and assurance about what we do not see" (Hebrews 11:1). As men of faith, we must take hold of this promise and live our lives with confidence and assurance in the God who has called us to be His children.

So let us be men of faith who live with intentionality, who surrender our lives to God's will, and who strive to grow in our relationship with Him each and every day. Let us be bold in our witness and unwavering in our convictions, knowing that God is faithful and will never leave us nor forsake us.

May we be known as men of faith who walk with purpose and passion, shining brightly in a world that so desperately needs the light of God's love and truth. May our lives be a testament to the power of intentional faith, and may we inspire others to do the same.

In the journey of faith, we all start as babes, filled with excitement and zeal for the Lord. We eagerly soak up His word, join in worship with fervor, and experience the joy of His presence in our lives. However, as we walk down the path of discipleship, we realize that our faith must mature and deepen in order to sustain us through the trials and challenges of life. In this chapter, we will explore the process of maturing in our faith and becoming men of faith who stand strong in the face of adversity.

The Foundation of Faith:

At the core of our faith journey is the foundation of our belief in Jesus Christ as our Savior and Lord. This foundation is the rock upon which we build our lives, and it must be solid and unshakeable. The apostle Paul writes in 1 Corinthians 3:11, "For no one can lay a foundation other than that which is laid, which is Jesus Christ." As men of faith, we must constantly reaffirm our commitment to Christ and seek to deepen our relationship with Him through prayer, study of the Word, and participation in the sacraments.

Growing in Knowledge and Understanding:

As we mature in our faith, we must also grow in
knowledge and understanding of the Scriptures. The
apostle Peter exhorts us to "grow in the grace and
knowledge of our Lord and Savior Jesus Christ" (2 Peter
3:18). We cannot remain content with a surface-level
understanding of the Bible, but must delve deeper into
its truths and apply them to our lives. This requires
discipline and commitment on our part, as we set aside
time each day to study and meditate on God's Word.

Developing a Spirit of Discernment:

One of the hallmarks of a mature Christian is the ability
to discern between good and evil, truth and falsehood.
The writer of Hebrews encourages us to "have your
senses trained to discern good and evil" (Hebrews
5:14). This means not being swayed by every wind of
doctrine or cultural trend, but standing firm on the
unchanging truths of Scripture. As men of faith, we
must be vigilant in testing every spirit and holding fast to
what is true.

Cultivating a Heart of Compassion:

As we grow in our faith, we must also cultivate a heart of compassion and love for others. Jesus tells us that the two greatest commandments are to love God with all our heart, soul, and mind, and to love our neighbor as ourselves (Matthew 22:37-39). This means reaching out to the poor, the marginalized, and the hurting in our communities, and showing them the love and compassion of Christ. As men of faith, we must be known not just for our beliefs, but for our acts of love and service towards those in need.

Standing Strong in the Storms of Life:

Finally, as men of faith, we must be prepared to stand strong in the storms of life. Jesus warns us that in this world we will face tribulation, but He also promises to be with us through it all (John 16:33). When the trials come – whether it be illness, financial hardship, or persecution for our faith – we must cling to the promises of God and trust in His sovereign plan. As the psalmist writes, "The Lord is my rock, my fortress and my deliverer; my God is my rock, in whom I take refuge" (Psalm 18:2).

The journey of faith Is not a sprint, but a marathon. It requires perseverance, discipline, and an unwavering commitment to Christ. As men of faith, we are called to grow stronger in our faith, deepen our knowledge of God's Word, develop a spirit of discernment, cultivate a heart of compassion, and stand strong in the storms of life. May we all strive to mature in our faith and become men of faith who bring glory and honor to our Savior, Jesus Christ.

In life, we all face storms. From the sudden loss of a loved one to the crushing weight of financial struggles, these storms can leave us feeling lost, alone, and broken. But as men of faith, we are called to weather these storms with unwavering trust in God's plan for our lives.

Throughout the Bible, we see examples of men who faced incredible trials and tribulations, yet remained steadfast in their faith. From Job, who lost everything he had but still praised God, to Peter, who walked on water in the midst of a storm, these men show us that with God, all things are possible.

One of the most famous stories of a man of faith facing a storm is that of Jesus calming the storm while out at sea with his disciples. In the Gospel of Mark, we read about how Jesus was in the boat with his disciples when a fierce storm arose. The waves crashed against the boat, threatening to capsize it, and the disciples were filled with fear.

But Jesus remained calm. He stood up, rebuked the wind and the waves, and said to the sea, "Peace! Be still!" And just like that, the storm ceased, and there was a great calm.

This story teaches us an important lesson about having faith in our storms. When we face trials and tribulations in our lives, it can be easy to give in to fear and doubt. We may feel like we are drowning in a sea of troubles, with no hope in sight. But just like Jesus calmed the storm for his disciples, he can calm the storms in our lives as well.

Having faith in our storms means trusting that God is in control, even when things seem out of control. It means believing that he has a purpose for our suffering and that he will bring us through the storm stronger and more resilient than before.

But having faith in our storms is not always easy. It requires us to surrender our fears and doubts to God and trust that he will guide us through the darkness. It means leaning on him in our weakness and allowing him to carry us when we feel like we can't go on.

One man who exemplified this kind of faith in the midst of a storm was the apostle Paul. In the book of Acts, we read about how Paul faced shipwrecks, beatings, and imprisonment for the sake of the gospel. Yet through it all, he never wavered in his belief that God was with him, even in the darkest of times.

In his letter to the Corinthians, Paul writes, "We are hard-pressed on every side, yet not crushed; we are perplexed, but not in despair; persecuted, but not forsaken; struck down, but not destroyed." These words remind us that even in the midst of our storms, God is with us, giving us the strength to endure and persevere.

As men of faith, we can take comfort in knowing that we serve a God who is bigger than any storm we may face. He is a God who calms the winds and the waves, who brings peace to our troubled hearts, and who carries us through the darkest of times.

So when the storms of life come crashing down around us, let us remember the example of the men of faith who have gone before us. Let us stand firm in our belief that God is with us, even in the midst of the storm. And let us trust that he will bring us through to the other side, stronger and more resilient than we were before.

For in the words of the psalmist, "God is our refuge and strength, an ever-present help in trouble. Therefore we will not fear, though the earth give way and the mountains fall into the heart of the sea." May we hold fast to this truth in the face of our storms, knowing that we serve a God who is always faithful, always true, and always with us.

Chapter 17

Embracing Obscure Faith

In the world of Christian faith, we often focus on the stories of great men and women who exhibited extraordinary faith in the face of trials and tribulations. We hear inspiring tales of individuals like Abraham, Moses, and David, who faced seemingly impossible circumstances with unwavering trust in God. However, what about those whose faith seems more hidden, more obscure?

In this chapter, we will explore the concept of obscure faith – faith that may not be as flashy or grand as the stories we often hear, but faith that is just as valuable in the eyes of God. We will look at how even in the midst of uncertainty and doubt, we can still trust in God and His promises.

The Bible is filled with stories of individuals who exhibited obscure faith. Take the story of Joseph, for example. Joseph was sold into slavery by his own brothers and unjustly thrown into prison. His circumstances seemed bleak and hopeless, yet Joseph remained faithful to God throughout it all. Despite his hardships, Joseph continued to trust in God's plan for his life and eventually rose to a position of power and influence in Egypt.

Another example of obscure faith can be found in the story of the widow who gave her last two coins to the temple treasury. In the eyes of the world, her offering may have seemed insignificant, but Jesus saw it differently. He commended her for her faithfulness and sacrificial giving, noting that she had given more than all the wealthy donors combined.

These stories remind us that faith does not always have to be visible or tangible to be meaningful. In fact, it is often in the quiet moments of uncertainty and doubt that our faith is truly tested and refined. As the writer of Hebrews reminds us, "Faith is the assurance of things hoped for, the conviction of things not seen" (Hebrews 11:1).

So how can we cultivate obscure faith in our own lives? One key aspect is learning to trust in God's sovereignty, even when we cannot see or understand His ways. In the book of Isaiah, God declares, "For my thoughts are not your thoughts, neither are your ways my ways" (Isaiah 55:8). We may not always understand why we are facing certain trials or challenges, but we can rest assured that God is in control and working all things for our good.

Another important aspect of cultivating obscure faith is learning to surrender our own desires and plans to God. This means letting go of our need for control and trusting that God's plans for us are better than anything we could ever imagine. As the psalmist writes, "Commit your way to the Lord; trust in him, and he will act" (Psalm 37:5).

Finally, cultivating obscure faith also involves seeking out community and support from other believers. We are not meant to walk this journey of faith alone, but rather in fellowship with one another. By sharing our struggles and doubts with others, we can encourage and uplift one another in our faith journey.

Obscure faith is a valuable and essential aspect of the Christian walk. It may not always be easy or glamorous, but it is in the moments of uncertainty and doubt that our faith is truly tested and refined. By trusting in God's sovereignty, surrendering our own desires, and seeking out community, we can cultivate a faith that is strong, resilient, and enduring. And like the men of faith who have gone before us, we can rest assured that God is faithful and will always be with us, no matter what lies ahead.

There are moments when our belief in God is put to the test. These are the times when we are faced with challenges, trials, and hardships that shake the very foundation of our faith. It is during these moments that our faith is tested and proven true.

The Bible is filled with stories of men who faced incredible trials of faith, but stood firm in their belief in God. One such man is Abraham, who was told by God to sacrifice his only son, Isaac. Despite the great promise God had given him about Isaac, Abraham obeyed without question, trusting in God's plan and provision. In the end, God provided a ram as a substitute sacrifice, proving Abraham's faith to be true.

Another man of faith who faced intense testing was Job. Job was a wealthy man who endured unimaginable losses, including the deaths of his children and the destruction of his possessions. Despite his suffering, Job remained steadfast in his faith, declaring, "Though he slay me, yet will I trust him." In the end, God restored Job's fortunes and blessed him abundantly, showing that his faith had been tested and proven true.

In the New Testament, we see the Apostle Peter's faith tested when he walked on water to Jesus. However, when he took his eyes off of Jesus and focused on the storm around him, he began to sink. Jesus reached out and saved him, but also challenged Peter's faith, asking him, "You of little faith, why did you doubt?" Peter's faith was tested on that stormy sea, but it was also strengthened as he learned to keep his eyes firmly fixed on Jesus.

As men of faith, we can expect our belief in God to be tested in various ways throughout our lives. It may be through financial struggles, health crises, relationship challenges, or persecution for our faith. These trials can either strengthen our faith or cause us to falter, depending on how we respond.

When our faith is tested, we have a choice to make. We can either cling to God and trust in His promises, or we can turn away in fear and doubt. The Bible tells us, "Consider it pure joy, my brothers and sisters, whenever you face trials of many kinds, because you know that the testing of your faith produces perseverance." We can choose to see our trials as opportunities for growth and refinement, knowing that God is with us every step of the way.

One of the key lessons we can learn from men of faith who have been tested is the importance of perseverance. Perseverance is the ability to endure hardships and trials with unwavering faith and trust in God. It is the willingness to keep pressing on, even when the road is rough and the future is uncertain. Perseverance is what separates those who give up in the face of adversity from those who stand firm in their faith.

The Apostle Paul wrote about the Importance of perseverance in his letter to the Romans, saying, "We also glory in our sufferings, because we know that suffering produces perseverance; perseverance, character; and character, hope." Paul understood that enduring trials and hardships was essential for building a strong faith and a deep trust in God.

As men of faith, we must cultivate a spirit of perseverance in the face of testing. We must remember that our God is faithful and will never leave us or forsake us, no matter how difficult the circumstances may be. We must hold fast to the promises of God's Word and stand firm in our belief that He is working all things together for our good.

When our faith is tested, we can take comfort in knowing that we are not alone. We have a great cloud of witnesses who have gone before us, men like Abraham, Job, Peter, and Paul, who have faced similar trials and emerged with their faith intact. Their stories serve as a reminder that God is faithful and just, and He will never let us down.

As men of faith, we will inevitably face trials and testing that will challenge the very core of our belief in God. These moments are opportunities for growth, refinement, and transformation. Through perseverance, trust, and unwavering faith, we can navigate these tests and emerge stronger and more steadfast in our walk with God. Let us learn from the examples of the men of faith who have gone before us, and may we too be found tested and true in our faith.

Faith is easy to have when life is going smoothly, when there are no storms on the horizon and everything is going your way. But true faith is tested in the fire of trials and tribulations. In the Bible, we see countless examples of men of faith who faced unimaginable trials and yet remained steadfast in their trust in God. In this chapter, we will explore some of these stories and draw lessons that we can apply to our own lives when we face inevitable trials of faith.

One of the most well-known stories of a man of faith facing trials is that of Job. Job was a wealthy man with a large family and many possessions. He was also a man of great faith, who honored God in all that he did. But one day, everything was stripped away from him – his possessions, his children, and even his health. Job's friends urged him to curse God and die, but Job remained steadfast in his faith, declaring, "Though he slay me, yet will I trust in him" (Job 13:15). In the end, God restored to Job double what he had lost, showing that even in the midst of trials, God is faithful to those who trust in Him.

Another example of a man of faith facing trials is that of Abraham. God called Abraham to leave his homeland and go to a place that He would show him. Abraham obeyed, even though he did not know where he was going. Along the way, Abraham faced many trials – famine, conflict with neighboring tribes, and the long wait for the promised son. But through it all, Abraham remained faithful, trusting in God's promises. And in the end, God fulfilled his promise to Abraham, making him the father of many nations.

The story of Daniel and his friends Is another powerful example of men of faith enduring trials. When they were taken captive to Babylon, Daniel and his friends faced pressure to conform to the pagan culture of their captors. They were tempted with rich foods and promised power and prestige if they would only compromise their faith. But Daniel and his friends remained steadfast, refusing to defile themselves with the king's food and instead choosing to trust in God. And in the end, God honored their faithfulness, blessing them with wisdom and favor in the king's court.

In each of these stories, we see a common thread – trials are inevitable for men of faith. Jesus himself warned his disciples that in this world they would have trouble, but he also promised to be with them always, even to the end of the age (Matthew 28:20). When we face trials, we can take comfort in knowing that we are not alone – God is with us every step of the way.

But how do we navigate these trials of faith? How do we remain steadfast in our trust in God when everything around us seems to be falling apart? The key is to remember who God is and what He has promised. The Bible is full of promises that we can cling to in times of trouble – promises of his love, his faithfulness, and his provision for our every need.

One of my favorite verses to cling to in times of trial is Psalm 46:1, which says, "God is our refuge and strength, a very present help in trouble." When we feel overwhelmed by the trials of life, we can take refuge in the arms of our loving Heavenly Father, knowing that He is our strength and our help in all circumstances.

Another key to enduring trials of faith is to surround ourselves with a community of believers who can support us and encourage us in our faith. The writer of Hebrews encourages us to "consider how to stir up one another to love and good works, not neglecting to meet together, as is the habit of some, but encouraging one another, and all the more as you see the day drawing near" (Hebrews 10:24-25). When we face trials, we need the support of our brothers and sisters in Christ to uplift us and remind us of God's faithfulness.

Finally, we must remember that trials have a purpose in our lives. James tells us to "count it all joy, my brothers, when you meet trials of various kinds, for you know that the testing of your faith produces steadfastness" (James 1:2-3). Trials can refine our faith, strengthen our trust in God, and ultimately bring glory to Him. As we persevere through trials, we can be confident that God is using them for our good and His glory.

Trials are inevitable for men of faith. But when we face trials, we can take comfort in knowing that we serve a faithful God who is with us every step of the way. By remembering His promises, leaning on our community of believers, and trusting in His purposes for our lives, we can endure trials with faith and perseverance. Like Job, Abraham, Daniel, and countless others before us, may we remain steadfast in our trust in God, knowing that He is faithful to those who love Him.

Through trials and tribulations, our faith is tested and refined, shining brighter and stronger for the world to see. As men of faith, let us embrace these inevitable trials as opportunities to grow closer to God, to deepen our trust in Him, and to bring glory to His name. May we stand firm in our faith, knowing that He who promised is faithful, and He will never leave us nor forsake us (Hebrews 13:5).

Chapter 18

Imperfect Yet Faithful

In a world that often emphasizes perfection and flawlessness, it can be easy to feel like we have to have it all together in order to have faith. But the truth is, faith is not about being perfect. In fact, some of the greatest men of faith in the Bible were anything but perfect. They made mistakes, they doubted, they struggled. And yet, their faith in God never wavered.

Take Abraham, for example. He was called by God to leave his home and travel to a land he had never seen. He was promised descendants as numerous as the stars in the sky, yet he and his wife Sarah were advanced in years and childless. Despite his doubts and fears, Abraham believed God and his faith was credited to him as righteousness.

Then there's Moses, who led the Israelites out of Egypt. He doubted his own abilities and questioned God's plan at times, yet he never lost faith in God's power and promises. David, a man after God's own heart, committed adultery and murder, yet he humbly repented and sought forgiveness from God.

The list goes on and on. Peter, Paul, Job, Jonah – all imperfect men who displayed unwavering faith in the face of trials and tribulations. They didn't have it all together, but they trusted in a God who did.

So what does this mean for us? It means that we don't have to be perfect to have faith. We don't have to have all the answers, we don't have to never doubt or never make mistakes. Faith is not about our own perfection, but about trusting in the perfect God who loves us unconditionally.

Just like the men mentioned in this book, you too can have that kind of mountain-moving, battle-ready faith. You can face your doubts and fears head-on, knowing that God is faithful and will never leave you or forsake you.

So let go of the pressure to be perfect. Embrace your imperfections and weaknesses, knowing that God's strength is made perfect in your weakness. Trust in Him, lean on Him, and watch as your faith grows stronger and bolder with each passing day.

Remember that faith is not about being perfect. It's about believing in a perfect God who is always at work in and through our imperfections. So go forth with confidence, knowing that you too can be a man of faith, just like those who came before you.

Remember that God used imperfect people for a perfect solution. It can be easy to get caught up in feelings of inadequacy and unworthiness, but the truth is that God has a plan and a purpose for each and every one of us. He chooses us for a reason, flaws and all, to bring about His perfect will in our lives and in the world around us.

One of the greatest examples of God using imperfect people for His perfect solution can be found in the Bible. Take David, for instance. David was a simple shepherd boy, the youngest of his brothers, and seemingly the least likely candidate to be chosen as king. Yet, God saw something in David that others did not. He saw a heart that was after His own, a heart that was willing to trust Him and follow His ways wholeheartedly.

David's journey was far from perfect. He faced many trials and tribulations, made mistakes, and sinned greatly. Yet, through it all, God remained faithful to him.

He used David in mighty ways, ultimately establishing him as a great king and a man after His own heart. David's story serves as a powerful reminder that God can use imperfect people to accomplish His perfect will.

Another example can be found in the apostle Peter. Peter was impulsive, outspoken, and often acted before thinking. He denied Jesus three times, yet Jesus saw something in Peter that others did not. He saw a man who would become one of the pillars of the early church, spreading the gospel to the ends of the earth.

Despite Peter's flaws, God used him in powerful ways. He preached boldly on the day of Pentecost, leading thousands to faith in Christ. He performed miracles, healed the sick, and even raised the dead. Peter's story is a testament to the fact that God can use imperfect people for His perfect solution.

So, what does this mean for us as men of faith? It means that no matter how inadequate or unworthy we may feel, God has a plan and a purpose for each of us. He has chosen us for a reason, flaws and all, to bring about His perfect will in our lives and in the world around us. We must have faith in what He can do through us, trusting that He will equip us and empower us to do great things in His name.

It is not our own strength or abilities that will bring about God's perfect solution, but rather our willingness to surrender ourselves to Him and allow Him to work through us. As we lean on Him and trust in His power, we will see miracles happen and lives transformed. We may not be perfect, but we serve a perfect God who can use us in incredible ways.

So, my fellow men of faith, remember that God uses imperfect people for His perfect solution. He chose you for a reason, so have faith in what He can do through you. Trust in His plan, rely on His strength, and watch as He works miracles through your life. You are not alone in this journey – God is with you every step of the way, guiding you, empowering you, and using you to bring about His perfect will. Embrace your imperfections, surrender yourself to His will, and watch as He works wonders through you. You are chosen, you are loved, and you are capable of great things in His name. Trust in Him, have faith, and watch as He uses you to bring about His perfect solution.

In times of uncertainty and doubt, it is so easy to falter in our faith and lose sight of the path that God has set out for us. As we navigate through the challenges and obstacles that life throws our way, it is vital to lean on God for guidance, strength, and direction.

Prayer For The Man Of Faith

Dear God,

I come before you today with a humble heart, seeking your guidance and wisdom. I acknowledge that I am not perfect, and I often veer off the path that you have set before me. I ask for your help in becoming a man of faith, one who trusts in your plan and walks in your ways.

Father, I know that faith is not just believing in you when things are going well, but trusting in your goodness and sovereignty even when the storms of life rage around me. Help me to have unwavering faith in your promises, knowing that you are always with me, even in the darkest of times.

Lord, I ask for your strength to resist the temptations and distractions that pull me away from you. Help me to prioritize my relationship with you above all else, seeking your will in all that I do. Let my faith be a shining light to those around me, that they may see your love and grace working in my life.

God, I pray for the courage to step out in faith, even when the path ahead is unclear. Help me to trust in your guiding hand, knowing that you will never lead me astray. Give me the courage to follow where you lead, even when it may be uncomfortable or challenging.

Lord, I ask for your grace and mercy when I fall short of being the man of faith that you have called me to be. Help me to learn from my mistakes and grow in my faith, trusting in your forgiveness and love.

Father, I surrender myself to you, asking for your guidance and direction in all areas of my life. May my faith in you grow stronger each day, as I seek to live a life that honors and glorifies you.

In Jesus' name, I pray, Amen.

As we seek to be men of faith, let us remember that God is always with us, guiding us, protecting us, and loving us unconditionally. Let us trust in his plan for our lives, knowing that he will never lead us astray. May our faith in him grow stronger each day, as we seek to walk in his ways and live out his will for our lives. Amen.

Letter To The Reader

Dear Reader,

I want to start by expressing my sincerest gratitude for taking the time to read this book. It means the world to me that you have chosen to invest your time and energy into learning more about the faith journey that I have shared within these pages. Your support and encouragement mean more to me than words can express, and I am truly thankful for your willingness to embark on this journey with me.

As you close the final pages of this book, I want to leave you with a message of encouragement and hope. I believe that each and every one of us has been called by God to be men of faith, to live our lives in a way that brings glory to Him and reflects His love and grace to those around us. I encourage you to embrace this calling with boldness and confidence, knowing that God has equipped you with everything you need to live out this calling.

Being a man of faith is not always easy. In fact, there will be times when you may face challenges and struggles that seem insurmountable. But I want to remind you that you are never alone in these moments. God is with you every step of the way, guiding and strengthening you as you navigate the twists and turns of life. Lean on Him in times of hardship, trust in His plan for your life, and know that He is always working for your good.

I also want to remind you that being a man of faith is not just about what you believe, but also about how you live out those beliefs in your day-to-day life. Let your faith be a light that shines brightly in the darkness, a beacon of hope and love for all those you encounter. Be quick to extend grace and forgiveness, slow to anger and judgment, and always ready to lend a helping hand to those in need. In doing so, you will be living out the true essence of what it means to be a man of faith.

In closing, I want to thank you once again for joining me on this journey. I pray that the words you have read in this book will inspire and challenge you to be the man of faith that God has called you to be. May you walk in His love and grace each and every day, and may you be a shining example of His goodness and mercy to all those you meet.

With heartfelt gratitude and blessings,

- Dr. Brandon Stewart